Amanda—
God Bless

TIFFANY
TWISTED

EXPOSED, *UNRAVELED,* REWRITTEN

TIFFANY TWIST

Andover, MN

ISBN 1-931945-17-9

Library of Congress Catalog Number: 2004107470

Printed in the United States of America

First Printing: June 2004

08 07 06 05 04   5 4 3 2 1

et al. Publishing
An imprint of Expert Publishing, Inc.
14314 Thrush Street NW,
Andover, MN 55304-3330
1-877-755-4966
www.expertpublishinginc.com

CONTENTS

PROLOGUE

～～～～～～

Spring 1975

Death sends for the commander of his army.

"Do you see that one there?" Death asks.

This commander called Pain, just back from a cold, dark mortuary, emerges with a satisfied smile on his face, his mind still relishing the sight of the bullet hole in his last victim's head.

Death's voice deepens, "Pain, are you listening to me?"

Pain shakes himself back to the present and looks toward the little girl, draws up his lengthy, scaly arm, and points.

"Her?" he asks.

"Yes," Death says, as he nods his head, his thumb and forefinger stroking his small, black pointed scruff on his chin, his black, beady eyes lit with greed.

A little girl sits content in the soft, green grass of earth, and rocks her baby doll. Little active fingers brush the baby's soft, blonde hair as she holds her up to the light of day and whispers, in seeming tranquility, a lullaby to her dolly, unaware of the rumble taking place overhead.

"Look at that kingdom around her," Death continues as he shakes his head in wonder.

It wasn't the grass or the little neighborhood in which she lived that his greedy heart desired. It was far beyond what mortal eyes could see.

"Absolutely extraordinary and I want it; I want those lands, and that castle…"

Pain looked at the little girl and saw what his master was talking about. He saw the potential, the call, the mighty destiny in this small person. And Pain knew his job. It was the same job he mastered many times over the years. He didn't get them all, but he got some and he savored every one.

"Get her for me," Death's voice trailed off with his footsteps.

Pain began his work immediately. He called in his troops with a roar, "Intimidation, Shame, Torment, Despair, we have work to perform."

Enemy soldiers filed into the room one by one and sat down at a massive, oak slab table. Each one slapped down a sheet of white paper in front of themselves and set about to work their separate evils.

They pondered the little girl in the grass and began to script her bondage—a script these enemy soldiers would spend years teaching her to believe—evils that, when unified, would orchestrate a living nightmare.

~~~~~~~~~~~~~~~~~~

Imagine your soul as a castle. Somehow, your fortress became penetrated. Weapons shot you down and the throne of your kingdom suffered invasion by an enemy.

Now this enemy, Pain, sits within your soul and battles to take it for his master, Death. You become blocked with arrows and bullets placed in the form of invasion, negative words, unfortunate circumstances, or possibly just a shrug of the shoulder, or a turn of the head.

When something strikes at you so hard it produces a negative feeling, don't falter. Be aware of the weapon and remove it. Identify the weapon coming from the enemy, and then identify the enemy. Is it a power-seeker such as Intimidation? Or is it a destiny thief such as Worthlessness, Shame, Guilt, or Low Self Worth?

Give yourself options, tools, and strategies. Understand what the battle is about. Your potential and your vision in life are the fuels you possess to reach your destiny. Your possibility and hope are the seeds that grow the fuel. Pain and Death want your land, your destiny. They call upon soldiers to work their harm. These soldiers set up incidents, through words and actions, to drain your fuel—your strength, your determination, your potential, and your vision. The success of Pain and Death come when you are without strength, without determination, and your possibility and hope—your seeds—are stifled from growth.

How do you fight? Stand strong, remind yourself why Death wants your castle—your life's call is great and your destiny threatens his very purpose in this world. Be aware of the significance of words and actions planted in your psyche by Death's soldiers, understand where they lead you, the state of mind they put you in, and you will have 90 percent of your battle conquered!

In this book you'll see the duel with Pain and triumph over Death through years of struggle with enemy soldiers and their weapons—sexual invasion, emotional abuse, abandonment, and rejection.

This book will drive you from victim to victor as you learn to find or take back the power in your life story, overcome enemy characters in your life, and script your freedom to reach your highest potential and your greatest destiny today!

ACKNOWLEDGMENTS

Many thanks to all of you who supported this work
with your kind words, patience, and love.

tif-fa-ny (tif′e nē)

n.

a thin gauze of silk or muslin.

twist′-ed

v.

to cause to take on moral, mental, or
emotional deformity.

~~~~~~~~~~~~~~~~~~~~~~

Behold,
I will bring it health and cure,
And I will cure them,
And will reveal unto them
The abundance of peace and truth.

—Jeremiah 33:6
KJV

~~~~~~~~~~~~~~~~~~~~~~

1 *the* HUNT

I thought about bringing a gun over there. Not just some little pistol. I had a statement to make. And a statement like this required one of those big shotguns, one that would bring hell itself into the eyes of its beholder.

I would drive up that street. I can't believe he still lives there. It's like triple torture knowing my stepbrother lives in the same house that holds the memories of what caused a lifetime of inner madness in me, torture knowing I could find him anytime my rage boiled beyond control, and torture knowing I could fulfill my dreams of revenge.

According to my fantasy, I pull up to that house, open the trunk, and remove "my statement." I walk slowly up the driveway.

I see a man slide out from under his car. I stop and take in his greasy hair, torn clothes, darkened teeth, and when I decide this is the grown version of my tormentor, I approach him and lift the long heavy barrel to his forehead, let him pause, then panic as his thoughts raced to who, why…?

Just then, like a sudden, unexpected wave, this dark scene I envision changes into another—a completely different scenario that plays out within my mind.

I see a little girl about five years old. She tosses a small rock into little chalked out squares on the sidewalk, and a little boy, maybe ten, as he plays catch with his dad. I see a beautiful woman, she stands in the doorway and wipes her hands on a dish towel, watches her family with a smile.

If I were to walk into this happy scenario, with despise in my eyes and a shotgun in my hands, I'd look like a crazed maniac. Part of me didn't care. But I let the gun slip from my hands and drop to the ground as I listened to the part of me that did.

Children?

The thought hadn't occurred to me before. Children being raised by a mad man?

I ask myself about the little girl in her pink dress and lacy socks with blonde curls bouncing up and down as she played hopscotch. Is she safe? Was he doing it to her?

I ponder the little girl and wonder how many adolescent sexual predators turn into adult predators and go on to abuse their own children. The thought makes me shudder and want to shoot him all the more.

But I'm not the murdering type. I must have learned somewhere along the line we aren't to kill other people out of anger, revenge, or any such emotion. I couldn't hurt anybody, not like that.

I would be more likely to turn the gun onto myself and kill the pain, not the cause.

It wasn't until after years of attempting to kill the emotional pain, without success, that I began to focus my anger on the cause with such fantasies of revenge and murder like the one before.

In the beginning, the cause of my emotional pain rarely even entered my mind—the brutality, the injustice. I only felt the pain, which was so strong it never let me get past it. The pain, the pain, the pain. Right there on top of the cause, hiding it, keeping it concealed like a huge, cement cover upon the soul. Heavy and overbearing, making itself so prominent, so strongly felt by the pain bearer, the cause goes unnoticed.

And if by chance the cause gets noticed, is recognized, or acknowledged, our beliefs about our situation or tormentor usually block any sort of process to healing. The hateful memories of the person or incident really only add bitterness to our soul, resentment to our core.

When we remember or fantasize about the tormentor or incident we relive the intimidation. We relive our powerlessness. We relive our helplessness. We relive our agony, and we stifle the very breath within our lives. We want to stay away from the memories and the hurt as long as possible, but by hiding, without searching, without rewriting, without changing our minds, we sit in anger and bitterness, we waddle in self loathing and self defeat, we forfeit happiness, we forfeit destiny, we forfeit life.

~~~~~~~~~~~~~~~~

A beast devours.
An animal
Takes what is not his.
Walks away,
Leaving his kill,
Shattered,
Torn,
Lifeless.

~~~~~~~~~~~~~~~~

2 *the* KILL

At first, in confusion over my emotions, I pacified my pain by smoking pot, sending my mind into a foggy haze, or drinking maybe a whole bottle of vodka, sending every nightmarish thought into oblivion.

If the vodka had killed me, I would have just been another teenager or young adult fallen to the arms of death in what they probably would have called some kind of accidental alcohol poisoning. And the truth—the truth that pain was my murderer—would have been hidden from the eyes of everyone who knew me and everyone who knew my family.

Driven to remove the pain, I tried to find a way to detach from it. I remember standing in a moment of hopelessness, crying over the bathroom sink. I slit the tips of each of my ten fingers with a razor blade.

I was sure the pain would flow out of me as I watched the drops of blood splatter against the white porcelain, mixing itself with the colorlessness of my tears pouring forth like a flood.

I focused on the pain. It consumed me, my life. I obsessively tried to find release, always searching for a way not to feel. And there seemed to be just a few ways I could accomplish a feelingless state. I found avenues for the despair and hopelessness to be conquered. Fantasies of death, daily drunkenness, or a drugged state seemed to be my most accessible options. But what I didn't understand was that through fantasies of death, drunkenness, or other self-destructive measures, hopelessness, and despair were not conquered at all, only pacified for a brief moment in time. In the morning, hopelessness and despair would rise along with me, eager to feed my pain and cause me to cry for its release once again.

I sat parked in my apartment garage with my car running, the exhaust pouring out around me. This time I had a piece of paper and a pen. I wrote down every reason I could not continue my life this way, how I could no longer wake up every day dealing this living, breathing occupant of my soul, this occupant called Pain. He made himself very large within me. He traveled from one place to another within me, from one memory to the next. He kept me stifled, hopeless, worthless, and was doing his work to bring me to a final conquered state of breathlessness, to fulfill his mission and remove life. Remove life, from me.

I liked the idea of a slow death, not acting out suicide on impulse, causing an irreversible action. I must have been present-ing my demise to an unseen God, a Ruler of the universe, hoping maybe he existed, was watching and cared. Trying to die slowly also gave me time to think, time to argue with the occupant, Pain, and time, with any remaining amount of strength, to ask this unwelcome trespasser, *who are you? What are you doing here—here in my life? Who invited you, and why won't you leave?*

I was trying to kill the pain and Pain, in his complete relent-lessness on my soul, mind, and body, was using me, using my physical body as a means to remove the earthly shelter my spirit inhabits. He was trying to kill me, unconcerned with my flesh life. He was after something deeper. He was after my very spirit, my soul.

This is Pain's long, repeated fight for the lives of his victims. He slips himself into our selves, our lives, usually at a young age, but not always, and slowly, through the years, becomes part of our identity, a part of our selves that we can no longer separate from the real us.

We come to believe we could never live apart from his torment. Not because we want to live with him, we just don't see the door we can open and we don't believe we can send Pain on his way. He makes himself appear all too powerful, and we who carry the pain feel too weak, too afraid to fight. Apart from fight there is only one other reaction—flight.

And as we try fleeing from ourselves, our very lives, too often we settle. Without tools, without searching, without understanding, we settle for unproductive methods of release—despair, depression, and worst of all, self-mutilation leading to self-murder.

I believed I could not kill the pain in my head, my heart, my soul, without killing my whole self. This is Pain's biggest deception. He wants us to believe he controls us; he is attached to us. He wants us to think he *is* us, and he cannot be conquered, ever, apart from the body, our body which he inhabits. Pain's master deception.

It happened this way with my second brother. He believed the pain. He didn't argue with the pain. He just took a pistol and put it into his mouth. Irreversible action. A murder wrought without justice. An assassin's job completed. He is Pain, with a smile of success as he gazes upon his dead victim, ready to turn and walk away, eager to conquer his next.

I stood over that lifeless body that lay upon the cold metal table and looked into my dead brother's face. I saw death. Death undefeated. Death with a final victory over a beautiful, sweet, wonderful young man. Pain had killed my brother. I knew this murderer. I realized his victory and I knew this Pain was the same occupant of my soul, the same one trying to take my life too.

As much as any of us would say suicide is death brought by one's own hand, we misunderstand. Pain commits this crime, and if I presented the case before a judge, accusing the true murderer, he, the murderer named Pain, would get off free, for all evidence would point to my brother's own hand holding that gun, and his own finger pulling that trigger.

As I recognized this murderer's presence in my own life and stood in that stark room with my brother's body, I called for a battle, a fight. I stood strong in an imaginary boxing ring within my head and called out loud for my opponent, Pain. He produced himself in his corner, laughing. He stood tall, strong, and ready for battle. I resolved to remain determined as a short, silent bell rang within my mind. And with that swift "ding, ding," I vowed not to stop until I knocked this enemy out of my life for good— and forever.

But at that moment, even with my new strength and resolve, I had no idea how many rounds it would take—the hours, the days, the years, the bruises, the cuts, the sweat, and the tears before I could claim victory.

It was a blessing to not know what I would have to endure to get to a place in which I could understand and embrace myself and my life. Had I seen it all ahead of time, I would have laid down and given up right then. I was thankful I just had to take this whole process of fighting my emotional pain small step by small step.

I fought little battles here and there. Little battles that added up to enemies conquered, a war won, and a land of peace and tranquility claimed. I learned to focus singularly on the small battle presented before me at the time it was presented and told myself I could find the strength to fight today and expect the victory would be mine. I learned I could fight hard today and rest tomorrow.

I crossed "lands" looking to the place where I would be free. And every land through which I passed presented a battle I needed to fight and an enemy I needed to conquer, so I could progress to the next land. Exhausting, and sometimes I felt my land of peace did not exist, but that was fear speaking to me. My spirit said, FIGHT!

The amazing part comes when we stand strong and determined through our small battles with Pain. Time passes and we accomplish distance. We look back upon the path on which we traveled and see our battlefields. Within those battlefields we see the places in our lives in which Pain and his soldiers—Guilt, Shame, Sadness, Regret, Self-hatred, Hopelessness—have been put down, slaughtered by our own determination to fight, once we finally decide to fight.

Only when we look at the full picture in the beginning of our quest and feel the power of the enemies as a whole, do we feel overwhelmed and defeated, feel our only choice is to surrender to death. We fall even before we have attempted to battle. This holds true with anything we are trying to overcome. We feel the defeat, sense the defeat, before we even begin to battle. Whether it is a terrible past, an addiction, a memory, or just an overwhelming to-do list, we look at the large picture, become overwhelmed, give in to our panic, and fall in surrender to the one we need to fight.

I see a winnable battle like this: In those karate type movies there is usually one good guy who has approximately fifty bad guys coming at him. Looking at the whole picture, we think there is no way one guy can succeed against fifty. It is logically impossible if all fifty fight. Then we see the one guy, not retreating in fear, not looking at the odds, not lying down to die, but methodically taking on one adversary at a time, watching and resting between enemy advances, preparing for the next one's attack. He continues his fight until all fifty are flat on the floor, defeated. And with this fearless, methodical approach, he keeps himself alive.

We, too, need to use a fearless, methodical approach to fighting our enemies in life, our memories, our addictions, our to-do lists. We cannot retreat in fear, and we cannot look at the odds, or the mass of people who seem to be against us. We cannot surrender and just lie down and die. We need to fight our adversaries one at a time, resting and watching between advances, until we sense the quietness and peace return, look back upon our battle, and smile upon our own enemies lying defeated, face down on the floor.

〜〜〜〜〜

How do I get to you?
Before you get to me?
Can I find your source of breath?
And cut it from my life?
Cast you out?
For good?
I shall resolve to never give up,
And in my weakness,
Reach out for strength,
Until you are gone,
Until you no longer breathe,
Within me.

〜〜〜〜〜

3 *the* VISITS

God used to visit me when I was a little girl. I would sense his presence. No one in my life really talked about him. At least not as if he was real and watching. I don't know who I thought he was or where he came from, but I knew he was there and I was safe when his presence filled my room.

He sat at my bedside with me, talked to me, and dried my tears. He touched my hands. They felt as if they became large and swollen. My fingertips felt tingly, and my physically-still hands sensed they were moving when he held them.

I remember no matter how agitated or upset I was, when my hands swelled I began to focus on them. Immediately, I became relaxed, even though I never really understood what was happening to me. I still don't understand it, but I know he was with me, promising that he would always be with me, that he would never leave me. He would never remove his quiet presence at my bedside holding my hands and bringing comfort to my little traumatized body and mind, offering hope, assuring peace.

He said things to me at my bedside. I wish I could remember them all. But I can't. I remember one thing, and I remember it as clear as day. I carried his promise through my years of childhood pain and adolescence trial, held somewhere in the recesses of my heart possibly because his promise was a piece of my future, something that would later bring me hope and purpose.

He told me I would be an author. I'm not sure if I asked or if He just said, "You will be an author." But for whatever reason, and the way he said it, I never told anyone.

It's funny he said it that way, "author." The word seemed so old and distinguished sounding. And not something a young child ever aspires to do. What do you want to be when you grow up? Doctor, teacher, nurse. You never hear a child say, "I want to be an author." Possibly this is a reason I never shared it with anybody. It sounded a bit odd, and I wouldn't have wanted to change his words that rang so clear to my young heart. It became our secret.

Even as I write this, pulling the memory from the depths of my soul was the first time I shared that story with my husband of ten years. He wasn't excited. He didn't even seem to care. Maybe that's another reason I never shared my secret with others. Who would have cared, or even believed me, for that matter?

I now imagine the amazing miracle of it all. God, the Creator of the universe, with nations and presidents, mass chaos, and destruction to worry about, sitting at a bedside of a teary eyed, lonely, scared little girl, and giving her hope with such an amazing vision of her future, her destiny.

I never really thought about it consciously again for years. For a long time his words, too, were buried deep with all the unhappy childhood memories I worked hard to keep far away from my surface thoughts, until the day I was ready to remember, ready to feel.

As I grew, I became too busy to listen to his voice. I have since quieted myself to hear him again. I once again experience the comfort he brings to his lonely, teary eyed children. And I once again reap the benefit his peace brings.

I am intrigued by observing others who keep themselves too busy, too preoccupied to hear his voice—this small, still, whispering voice that speaks to the hearts of his creation.

People filled with unhappiness, unsettled agitation, having no real clarity of who they are or who they should become. They fill their lives with noise, busyness, and distraction, anything that drowns out the voice that brings direction and hope.

And they do this, for one of two reasons: pain or fear.

We fill our lives with garbage such as addictions, busyness, or preoccupation to cover up the pain. Pain's loud bellowing causes us to deal with him, and with that, we drown out the small, still voice that comforts, that helps us deal with Pain so we may be set free in a truly liberating way, one without addiction and unsettling busyness—a way in which we are truly be able to be free, to relax, and to enjoy life the way life was meant to be enjoyed.

We also may drown out the voice of God out of fear—fear of hearing direction, fear of being told the path we are on is wrong. Because we fear the unknown, the more difficult, and the more challenging, we consciously drive the voice of direction away through our busyness. We push God's comforting voice far away from us with the television, the radio, the phone calls.

When this is so, when we try to ignore the voice of peace or drown out the voice of direction, things may go really wrong in our lives. Circumstances may get really bad and hopeless. But this is God's mercy for our lives that have gone awry. His mercy is telling us we are going the wrong way, telling us we are about to be defeated by someone or something. A place of turmoil is the only place we get desperate enough to desire his answers. Once we are amidst the turmoil we need to get quiet and listen to our Commander. He will give us the battle plan. And it will always be one in which you will be the victor. When God calls for a battle, he has already planned the victory. It may not look like what you would have expected, but be assured that somewhere, within or without, victory ensues.

~~~~~~~~~~~~~~~~~~~~~~~~~~

A knowing.
A knowing when nothing else can be known,
When nothing else makes sense,
But this one thing,
That shouldn't make sense,
But does.

~~~~~~~~~~~~~~~~~~~~~~~~~~

4 *the* DUST

I look back to view my childhood as empty, miserable, my mind as a blank slate. I had a lot of things I didn't want to think about, and thus cleared my small mind of everything. I just existed, sort of half way, half living, not consciously feeling.

Later in life members of my family accused me of focusing on the bad, and suggested I think of the good times in my childhood because there were good times. I'm sure there were.

But to find the good in my childhood meant sifting through the bad, like finding a needle in a haystack. And to get to that needle I would have to get my hands filthy in the hay. I would have to look at it, touch it, weed through it, breathe its dust, cough, and gag upon it. It wasn't worth it to me. I wanted to just turn away and never look back.

When I was asked a question or told a story that reminded me of something from my past, the voices sent a cold chill down my spine; the demands and pressure to remember began to torment me.

"Turn around look at the haystack, don't you remember that needle?"

Torment. Don't they know it's painful to remember.

No. I won't turn around, I won't look at it. It hurts to even try and see that little girl.

"What is wrong with her? Why do you do this to us every time? She's crazy, always wanting sympathy or something. Get over it."

The inner tears began to fall.

Get over it? Tell me now, how do you get over a massive, dirty, dusty pile of hay and not sink with the first two steps, only to stab a needle into your foot?

———~~~———

Can't you see,
I choose to live with my eyes shut?
I need my lids to cover their sensitive tissues.
For when you make me open them,
When you make me see,
They burn,
They sting,
They water.

———~~~———

5 *the* DISEASE

Who would know that sexual abuse would be like a contagious, infectious disease, leaking itself into every cell of my body, spreading itself through every day, week, and year of my life, affecting my decisions, my thoughts, and actions?

It wasn't a physical disease, but it felt like one. And worse. I couldn't just go to a doctor, be diagnosed, and treated. It felt as if some dreadful cancer visited my life and deposited its evil droppings within my very being. Not a physical disease, it was sexual abuse, a different sort of disease that carries with it symptoms like shame, embarrassment, low self worth, and guilt that affect the lives of those it infects. Symptoms that need to be identified and dealt with one by one, as soldiers on a battlefield.

Someone who hasn't been abused, who has not suffered through repeated incidents may not understand. They may say, "If the cause is gone, if the disease is taken care of, then the pain should go away also."

This may be so with disease or sickness of the flesh, but not with a disease that has invaded your soul.

The cause may be gone, but your soul never forgets. The cause embeds and permanently damages, more like a disease of the womb—a womb altered somehow, not shaped as it should be for a growing baby. The cells of the baby are growing, forming in this misshaped womb, being attacked by the disease that's pushing them to places they were not meant to be, mutilating the transformation of this vulnerable, growing human.

Months go by. The baby leaves the tormentor womb. Leaves the disease behind and comes out deformed. Marked. Scarred. The quiet laughter of the disease continually ringing in the ears of the newly mutilated person the disease has preyed upon.

And once we view this deformity, we cannot push the cells back into place; the cells remain where they have been positioned, for that is their job, to remember and stand fixed.

And so the womb, the tormentor, does what it is being used for. It brings to its victim a life just short of wholeness and completion, perfection never brought into existence. A victim can choose to mask his pain, cover his mutilation, but life will never be as it could have been. The cells stand strong beneath the mask and mutilation exists beneath its chosen covering and the victim remains with a deep, hidden knowledge of his deformed state, his reasons for being covered, his purpose for hiding.

Mutilation of the soul comes from being repeatedly violated in the innocence of childhood, shameful mutilation commanding to be hid, to be covered, to be kept in secrecy.

We find the masks, the covering, and anything else we can use to hide our guilt and our shame. But why? What do I have to be ashamed of? I was a little girl who asked for none of what was done to me.

If adults who knew first hand about shameful sexual acts committed on innocent, unknowing children, and a society who doesn't want to confront such injustice, became a voice so loud it couldn't be ignored, maybe then abused children could be saved.

Why couldn't my own mother have saved me? She was no stranger to this disease; she carried Pain's burdensome secrets from her own childhood. She chose the mask, chose her covering, and chose not to open her eyes to the possibility of such cruelty being inflicted upon and endured by her own young daughter.

I wonder, do we somehow think sexual invasion a game of chance, a happening just a part of life to be tolerated? Or is it just inevitable as we can't glue our eyes to our children twenty-four seven and it is bound to happen sometime, somewhere, somehow, to someone's child? Maybe once or twice, but eventually the symptoms to this disease will become apparent, and if we are aware, as parents, teachers, guardians, caregivers, doctors, aunts, and uncles, we can stop the enemy from gaining control over, and bringing a lifetime of torment to, such a vulnerable human being.

I don't want a mask. I want to confront my Pain and heal from it, kick that unwelcome occupant from my life. I want to do the best I can to protect my children from sexual injustice happening to them. Ignorance is bliss, they say. For whom? Definitely not for the children.

Look, look at my scars. If you want to look at me you have to accept the scars of my disease. If you don't want to look at my scars, then I don't want you to look at me. If you hurt to look at them, imagine how I feel, the one cursed to wear them.

Only when I look at my own scars can I really feel for other scar bearers, only when we all look at our own deformities can we have compassion and will to fight, to stop the disease from spreading, and to save the children from Pain's mutilating effects.

~~~~~~~~~~~~~~~~~~

Oh, Lord.
The spots upon my soul,
Intruding, dark, foreign.
Why have they been placed just so,
But to make me cry,
To the very depths of my spirit.
Will all my tears wash them away?

~~~~~~~~~~~~~~~~~~

6 *the* PURPOSE

I ran into a girlfriend one day whom I see only periodically, maybe a few times a year. We chatted about the warm weather and work. We connected with silent words from the heart that spoke—*yes, I remember our visits; we are friends, I can talk with you*—and our conversation quickly turned meaningful.

This girl was shaken. Her face filled with sadness as she told me she struggled to confront her childhood abuse. Sharing is what comes from tearing off the mask, from refusing to wear a mask, from opening up and refusing to hide the secrets tearing us up inside. We scar bearers speak to each other.

She spoke with her own family about her memories, her pain, and they rejected her—mom, dad, sister. They were all unwilling to look at her scars.

Rejection turns its head away when the scar bearer is really just asking, "Will you still love me with my scars? Because I don't know if I should love me with these scars, and I need your help."

Like my friend, I, too, needed an answer to those questions. Questions my family mistook for, "*Look at me, look at my scars, don't you pity me?*"

Please understand. It is love we ask for—not pity—love, understanding, and acceptance. If this step of acceptance and love can be gained by a scar bearer, it will propel them into a state of healing.

If we are accepted and loved by others first, we can easily learn to love and accept ourselves. But considering acceptance is not easily found in a world of selfishness and judgment; we must travel another road when our hearts ask for healing. This road is a road paved with difficult, rocky terrain. It is a path in which love and acceptance must be gained by one's *own self*. With love and acceptance of self, the world's view of us no longer matters, no longer hurts, no longer provides a weapon we can use to slaughter our selves, our self worth, and our hope.

We need to know it is rare to find acceptance outside of ourselves. Unconditional acceptance happens to very few gifted, fortunate children. Many children are emotionally battered and beaten, or just simply ignored, verbally or nonverbally given the message they are worthless and unimportant.

Once we realize that value is not going to come from outside of us, we need to decide to look within. We take the power from others to define us and use the power to define our own selves, apart from the opinion of others.

Defining our life for ourselves is the mindset that separates the conqueror from the conquered, the successful from the defeated. Taking back our power severs fear, poverty, and death, and brings courage, riches, and life.

So, with a turn of their heads, this family symbolically told my friend her scars were too ugly to look upon, so ugly and repulsive they should be covered up and denied, not even mentioned. As she looked outside herself for acceptance and was denied, she found herself covered so completely with rejection that she felt imprisoned, twisted in her tiffany mummy-like wrappings forever.

She suffered rejection through not understanding—not understanding the pain, the disease, the mutilation of the victim.

Her family expected her life should be carried on, denying the sadness, away from the cause, apart from her abuser.

What a terrible emptiness the soul carries when you are rejected by those closest to you, by the ones placed on earth to love you and nurture you, but instead, who wrap you up like a mummy. Covering you. Denying you. How do you heal if your wounds are given no air?

〜〜〜〜〜〜〜〜〜〜〜

My wounds are soft, open.
The wrappings brush their surface,
Reminding me they are there.
Not seen, but felt.
A forgetting moment passes,
Until I make a wrong move,
Just right,
I cry out.
My wounds are soft, open.

〜〜〜〜〜〜〜〜〜〜〜

7 *the* FEAST

I was told later in life that sexual abuse was not something you talked about in the seventies. It was masked, covered up. Those sexual predators really had it made. No one spoke about what they were doing, the lives they were capable of destroying. No one talked about it, no one taught about it. Not even a mother spoke about it with her own child.

Not even a mother who experienced it herself.

A society of people who should know better—aunts, uncles, parents, teachers—opening up the children of the world and setting a tempting feast before any and every predator. What kinds of people place their children on a platter, stuff a piece of fruit in their mouths, and set them on a table before a drooling, perverted beast?

It's not like the adults couldn't have known. Maybe they should have asked. They chose not to know. Or ask.

Was it ignorance? Was it choice? Was it embarrassment? These are painful questions to ask. What was it that made my mother not care? What about my dad or anyone else in my life? What made anyone not ask about the teary-eyed secluded little girl? It is hard to feel unloved, unworthy of a safe, happy life.

Why did I have to live this way? Why did all this need to be happening to me? Why do I have to be unworthy of safety and happiness?

Where was everyone? Why didn't they wonder and ask themselves, "let's see, why is it she screams and cries not to be left alone with that sweet young man?"

~~~~~~

The eyes of a child speak.
Is anyone listening?

~~~~~~

8 *the* ADULTS

School never provided a place of refuge. I didn't enjoy it very much. I didn't fit in. I harbored secrets I couldn't talk about with anyone—secrets that caused me to feel out of place, different, unworthy. I didn't trust adults anywhere. I respected them to a certain extent, once I felt they weren't going to hurt me, but even then I remained cautious. The fallacy of adults confused me; their knowledge of life's rules was inconsistent.

I knew they weren't going to help me. I knew they couldn't help me. I realized much later in life adults were just a bunch of bigger kids, with real money, running around in the world.

No one really ever grows up and understands life. No one really has all the answers and the power to protect. I remember turning thirty, with children of my own and thinking, *this is what it's like to be an adult? I'm thirty, an adult, and I don't know sh--!*

Games.

That's what adults played. Running around their lives pretending they knew what they were doing, when the higher percentage of them didn't. And that's what my young life contained, adults who pretended and caused confusion for my young growing mind.

Confusion, like Santa Claus, the Easter bunny, God, angels, tooth fairy, boogey man, and any other of the characters we are taught to cast in or out of the scripts we are beginning to write as a child.

The casting for my script looked something like this.

Santa was this big fat red suited man who could get into my house every winter. Strangers we avoided; we were to beware of anyone we didn't know or our parents didn't know. But Santa, he wasn't a stranger. Although I never really saw him, he was welcome into our home every winter, to sneak around in the middle of the night. And we sat on the friendly fat man's lap Christmas season in the mall. Kind of ironic it was a different lap every year, a *stranger's* lap. It surprises me that more predators aren't running around in Santa suits. What an easy in we've given them to get their plattered feast! Confusion and more confusion.

During grade school age I figured this all out. I gained much knowledge about the deception that my parents engrained into my young mind the first six years of my life. First of all, upon learning the truth about these characters my parents taught me to cast, I felt it was completely acceptable to lie and manipulate any situation I chose over anyone I chose. Second, I learned to never trust what any of these big people told me, I'd find out later it was a lie.

Did they not understand I would have a hard time believing what I couldn't see including a protective God and his fighting angels after being burned with the realization of the rest of my parent's deception? How could *they* punish me for lying, telling me it is wrong, when they spent the first six years of my life showing me it is acceptable, appropriate, even fun, to lie and deceive?

We went to church. We learned about God and his angels. I never saw them, but was taught to believe in them just like I was taught to believe in a fairy I never saw every time I lost a tooth, or a bunny every time I found a basket.

Do we ever ask ourselves if, for a child, we are sabotaging a real relationship with an unseen God when an unseen bunny is revealed as entertaining deception?

It happened that way for me; from that point on it seemed I was all alone in the world. It was all confusion, fallacy, and still more confusion.

Then we have the boogie man, bad guys, whatever you want to call them. The adults in my life tried to convince me they did not exist. Fallacy, because the fact is, in my life, there *was* a boogey man, but if I tried to talk about him, the adults would tell me that there is no such thing, that I shouldn't be so afraid. They were certain of this. My parents didn't see what I saw. My little sister, who shared my room, didn't see what I saw. They didn't see the dark, skinny figure standing in my doorway of my little bedroom commanding me to come with him.

Lies, confusion, and deception coming from those adults whose authority and superior knowledge I needed to live under, those adults who cared not for the understanding, the wisdom, security, and safety my young heart longed for. No wonder so many children grow into lying, screwed up adults, and start the process once again with the next generation.

〜〜〜〜〜〜〜〜〜〜〜

Upon whom may I rely?
Upon whom can I set my heart?
It seems no one is willing.
I must grip it tightly to myself.
Hide it.
Keep it safe.
And give it to no one.

〜〜〜〜〜〜〜〜〜〜〜

9 *the* REBELLION

I lived every day with both of my parents for the first few years of my young life until we children were taken from my dad. After that he became somewhat of a stranger to me. He never talked much. My dad was a man of very few words, which can be a positive thing. He offered very little criticism or judgment when it came to our family. And after what my mother had done to him, I'm sure he could have spoken many words of criticism and judgment. He did not. He kept quiet and stayed out of our lives twenty-six days a month.

It seemed I didn't know him all that well. After the divorce, my dad was gone, and I was never assured of his concern for me. He had little to say to a five-year-old girl he didn't know all that well. He was a stranger who picked me up at a specified meeting place with my mother. They spoke not a word to each other as they transferred the little pink and blue flowered suitcases from my mother's trunk to my dad's.

As we pulled from the curb, I watched my mother get into her car and disappear into some kind of distant freedom. When I lost sight of my mother, I focused my attention on this man who was continually monitoring the speed of his car. I watched him lift his hand on the steering wheel every so often to view the dash and keep the little red needle where it needed to be. I studied every move he made and tried to convince myself he was my daddy.

I scanned every landmark I could remember from the previous trip that brought me to his house two weeks earlier. If he took a different route I became very fearful that he was not my daddy I was riding with.

I concentrated hard on his face just where the hairline met his skin, looking for any lines to convince me he was an imposter covering his real face. I thought at any minute this possible intruder would stop the car, tear away a mask and reveal himself as a monster, and hurt me. It seemed I was always fearful of someone bigger than me, taking me in my childhood weakness, taking me over, hurting me, making me cry and hate my very existence.

My own sadness caused me to be like my daddy when I was young. I stayed in the shadows. Not seen, not talking, not heard, so as not to be noticed by anyone who could hurt me. I hid, and I kept myself as isolated as possible.

That was until I was older, until I "rebelled." That is what society calls it. As soon as I became more aware of myself as a person, around fourteen, I began to unwrap myself from my mummy-like state. That's what the parents, the teachers, and the counselors called what I was doing—rebellion. It was that simple, I was tagged and diagnosed by oh, so intelligent people. How ignorant they were.

Why didn't they realize rebellion was a symptom of a sick, diseased person crying out for help? Why didn't they understand nothing changes with the disease if they only treat the symptom?

But the symptom was what they treated, thus bringing detentions, suspensions, grounding, and ridicule. Unfair discipline is what happened when I started to unwrap the tiffany and show the scars no one wanted to gaze upon.

"Rebellion! What do you think you are doing? Keep quiet. You're too young to know what you are talking about."

I'm just trying to be set free.

"Rebellion is not tolerated here. Speaking out is not tolerated here. You will obey the rules and keep quiet. Your opinion doesn't matter. Your concern is not welcome. We don't have time to deal with your trivial life events. Just wait and see what you have in store for you in the real world. Be neither seen nor heard. Go to your room. Your presence carries rebellion. Your voice holds rebellion."

How is it rebellion?

"Why, those mummy wrappings must stay on. We all have our own troubles and cannot be concerned with yours. Those wrappings must stay on."

Says who? They are tight, uncomfortable. I just can't stand them anymore. I just need to loosen them a little.

"Rebellion! Go to your room. I cannot bear to look at you without your shroud."

And so I am tagged. And because they can no longer confine my body behind the wrappings, they begin to confine my life.

~~~~~~~~~~~~~~~~~~~

It is as a dream,
I want to speak,
I cry to speak,
But the words carry no sound.
Help me, help me,
I scream,
But no heads turn,
No ears hear,
No arms are wrapped around me.

~~~~~~~~~~~~~~~~~~~

10 *the* ARTICLE

My dad always took me to the doctor, never my mother. Strange thing since I didn't even live with him. He always took me to the dentist, too. I'm not sure why that is, maybe because he had the insurance. I'll just leave it at that.

I later wished he would have talked more, been more judgmental and critical, given me some kind of clue the things going on at my mother's second husband's house were destructive. I hated living with Trucker Tom and his crazy son, my tormentor—living with the drunkenness, the fighting, the abuse, the being left alone.

I wished my dad would have been more nosey and investigative about what my mom was doing and what kind of things were going on at our house. But I guess it was none of his business, that by being nosey. He would somehow betray the wonderful, lovely new wife in his life. If my dad was anything, he was a devoted and faithful man in the sanctimonious bond of marriage.

I later pondered what might have happened had the phone rung while my stepbrother, my tormentor, engaged me in my torturous ritual. *Would my daddy have demanded to speak to me? If I had been crying would daddy have raced over without lifting his hand from the steering wheel to check his speed? Would he have sent the police?*

I wished it had, but it never happened that way. I glanced over at the man who had no idea who I was or how twisted my insides really were.

Together we waited patiently in those square upholstered lobby chairs for my name to be called, to go into the office for a physical or some general procedure. My daddy sat to my left and tables of magazines lay spread out on a little table to my right. Small children played with blocks on the floor in front of me. Ringing phones demanded to be answered, sick people checked in and out, nurses busied themselves behind their station.

I began to get bored with my thoughts and all the activity around me, so I looked down at the table on my right. My eyes searched for some type of entertainment in the magazine pile. My arms were lazy, so my eyes did the work.

As it goes with fifteen-year-olds, I had no interest in picking something up to read, especially something like a boring magazine article with so many words and all those paragraphs. So the bright pink square box highlighted in the corner of an open magazine caught my eye. It was titled, "Symptoms of Sexual Abuse."

~~~~~~~~~~~~~~~~

A place inside of me speaks.
It is time…
No, don't tell her, she will cry.
It is time…
But we've worked so hard to keep her safe.
It is time…
Well, if you say it is time…
Then, fine, it is time…

~~~~~~~~~~~~~~~~

11 *the* FIRST SYMPTOM

It was a list of probably five or six of these "symptoms." (Imagine, *symptoms*, like with a sickness or a disease.) Anyway, I can't remember them all. Some fit; others I may not have gotten to quite yet, like promiscuity, for example.

Rebellion may have been on the list. If rebellion wasn't on the list, it probably should have been. Why should such a powerful symptom get away with being overlooked?

Peeing the bed struck me. It had been such an embarrassment to me as a girl. I was as secretive as I could be, not waking anyone when I woke to realize I had just peed my bed. It's very traumatizing for a child to know they are different, that his or her friends can go on sleepovers, but they can't for fear of wetting in someone else's house.

I remember being nine or ten waking to the soppiness beneath me. I would quietly get up in my drowsiness and set out to the hall linen closet, grab the thickest towel I could find and place it over "my symptom," my mark of freakazoidness. And I would go back to sleep. This was a regular ritual and nobody ever thought to ask why. They just threw it in my face, taunting me, it felt, as if I, as a small girl, could control a symptom that was a branch of my unknown disease. The nightly dialogue was torment.

"Make sure you go potty now, you know how you pee the bed."

I would go potty. I would still pee the bed.

"Oh, little girl, you wet the bed again? Didn't you go potty before you went to sleep?"

Of course I did, I was a very obedient child at that age, and I was just probably so scared that monster would come into my room—or maybe my tormentor inhabited my dream—I peed.

This was especially embarrassing if it happened at my dad and stepmom's house. My heart sinks when I replay the memory of her scrubbing out the mattress with vinegar water. The smell haunts me. All I could do was watch her, be sorry I was alive to cause this extra work for her, and cry.

～～～～～～～～～～

Does anyone know what is wrong with me?
Can anyone tell me why?
I just don't understand, why me?
Why me?

～～～～～～～～～～

12 *the* SECOND SYMPTOM

Another symptom that jumped out at me was the compulsive masturbation symptom. As a small child, I wouldn't have known what that was, but at fifteen, I knew.

I knew enough to know that playing with yourself was dirty, secret. I'm not sure where I learned that, or if I just knew, but considering we are born blankly into the world, I must have learned it.

It's possible I could have been caught somewhere along the line and told it is wrong to play with your private areas. But being that it became a compulsive obsession for me starting around the age of six, I lived with it unexplained, believing I was a nasty, dirty, marked child.

I remember the way the adolescents who were figuring all this sex stuff out would laugh about the whole idea of masturbation in their secret little circles when no adults are looking.

But the difference between the two perspectives is the way someone laughs and makes comments at a bald man whose normal life process causes him to lose his hair and someone pointing and laughing at someone who has lost her hair to cancer: same baldness, yet one natural, one a symptom of disease. If kids were laughing or making comments about masturbation around me, they were pointing at my cancer.

I sat in that doctor chair pondering that "symptom" and remembered my hiding spots. Even obvious ones like the living room floor, watching the television. I would prop a small fort with an umbrella and a blanket, and do it right there, head and feet exposed, but the busy middle hid from sight. As young as six years old, I experienced orgasm after orgasm until I thought my pounding heart would give way, and I would die. I would climax, count the thumping beats until my heart calmed, and go back to work. It was yet another way I attempted slow suicide. I imagined, *well, after fifty orgasms in a row, thirty eight minutes of compulsive masturbation, her little heart just couldn't handle any more. The girl passed with one final climax…*

I really did think I would die from all that, but it still didn't keep me from visiting that spot I wished I hadn't known so much about until later in life.

My symptoms. Maybe missed, maybe passed over. Strange sexual behavior from a child needs to be investigated. Excessive self play, using objects to stimulate, or for penetration, uninhibited grabbing the crotch of others, terrifying fear to be alone with another adult, for example, should all be looked into.

If a child has symptoms of fever, runny nose, stomach cramps, we investigate the illness. We ask where it hurts, how bad it hurts, then go to the doctor. We diagnose the flu, then take steps to ease those symptoms and cure that sickness.

Awareness is the most important key to identifying this illness of sexual invasion, this disease of sexual abuse.

Why hadn't anyone noticed that my hair was falling out? I imagine my mother, "oh, another clump of hair." Thinking, just natural loss, it must be in the genes, guess she'll be a baldy.

No, mom. It's cancer.

And it's eating me alive.

~~~~~~

Who is this?
Controlling me?
Who takes over my thoughts?
My actions?
What am I doing?
And why am I doing it?
Are the decisions mine?
Or are they coming from outside of me?
Who will answer?
And tell me who I am.

~~~~~~

13 *the* REVELATION

The deception of my secrecy began to fade; somewhere deep inside a voice emerged, trying to speak, the words beginning to form, and the explanation ready to come forth. I realized mine were not normal childhood behaviors, and a door opened. At fifteen, I began to realize some of the truths of my childhood.

I remember exactly where and how it all came back.

I spent the summer before my entrance into high school at my dad's hanging out with friends, watching movies, listening to music, just walking around, hanging outside the drug stores, the ice cream shop, etc.

There was this guy, and I really liked him.

He was tall for his age, which, by the way, was a few years older than mine. Unbelievably built for a teenager, he had this tight little hairy butt (maybe where I acquired my taste for "monkey butts" as someone once called them in trying to defend his own baby smooth one). Note to the smooth one: Yours is really nice, too; even without hair, I am intrigued.

Anyway, this hairy butt guy, he had the tan muscular skin, the bluest eyes, the perfect name, and he wanted me. Little, dorkey me.

I just started to come out of my awkward pre-teenage ugliness that summer. I traded my ugly glasses for contact lenses, vowing to never wear those third and fourth eyes ever again. To this day only about four people have seen me in those obtrusive make-you-ugly-in-a-second-just-watch-as-I-put-them-on things. I don't mean to offend, it is just what I look like in eye glasses, and I believe there are people who look great wearing them.

What else? I was shaving my legs and shaving my pits, putting on suntan oil, fixing my hair, wearing make-up. In other words, I was learning how to make myself look good. Even though hairy butt guy didn't see me as dorkey on the outside, I was still very awkward on the inside.

This boy and I made ourselves comfortable on the multicolored shaggy carpet of my dad's basement family room. The smell of suntan oils filled the room as he got me naked. Anyway, we tried. It didn't work. His oversized semi was much, much, much too large for my little virgin garage. So we improvised. And you know what?

It was like disease meeting pain. Like, (sing this part) *Here I am, your tormentor, staring you right in the face. HA, HA, HA. I am the one. The cause.*

There it was, my cancer. An organ I knew. Back to haunt me. This organ, familiar, not foreign as it should have been with my first experience. And I was entertaining it. Here, let's mesh, mold together. And I was asking my cancer for more. More pain, misery, and destruction to bestow upon my life.

That was the day. The day it all came rushing back into the forefront of my mind. I later lay alone in my daddy's basement. Horrible, painful visions fought to be revealed. I see the bed. I see the bedspread, its colors, patterns, the tassels that hung to the carpeted floor.

I see him, my tormentor, lying upon that bed—and I hear my stepbrother, his instructions to go to the bathroom and get the Vaseline.

I feel, also, as I see that little girl in the doorway, I feel very small—very afraid—it's going to hurt. I feel my heart pounding.

I see him waiting, spread naked upon that bed—bigger than me—stronger than me—commanding me.

I hear, too. I hear my mother's instructions to be good and to be obedient to the one whom she has left in charge, the one she entrusted her precious little daughter to.

Her voice echoes as she sneaks out the door to go to a bar with her boozer husband, or maybe without, maybe to meet someone else.

"Listen to what he says, he's in charge, go to bed when he tells you, do what he tells you to."

Do what he tells you to?

And just like that I was placed upon a platter, a piece of fruit stuffed in my mouth, and set on a table before a drooling, perverted beast.

Trying to push the horror away, I curled up and soaked the carpet with my tears, picked up the phone, and called my daddy.

The sleeping beast,
Awakened,
He lives to torment me in my memories.
He breathes to make me hate my life.
His heart beats to remind me.
Remind me of my shattered, unclean state.

14 *the* COUNSELORS

So, what do good parents do with a rebellious, sexually active teenager upon discovering her childhood abuse? Take her to the family counselor, of course.

This began my repulsion for counselors. They didn't help me. They didn't keep my second brother alive. They didn't keep divorce from my family. Who were these people?

I do not doubt there are true people of wisdom out there. But I bet they are extremely rare. Extremely. Mine was one of the many who occupy the yellow pages, doctors' offices, mental health facilities, and wherever else they make themselves known.

A desk, a few chairs, a degree on the wall, and stacks and stacks of books that tell how to get into a person's head. Zilch for experience. Nothing. No "been there, experienced that, came through it, healed from it, and can help you through it, too." Nothing like that. Just book knowledge. Counseling is just a lot of, "Why are you doing what you're doing?" This is a symptom question, trying to analyze the symptom or treat the symptom. I answer them, we talk about the abuse for a moment, but they sit there with no idea of what to do about it, so continue with the symptom analysis, "Why can't you stop rebelling and doing what you are doing?"

"I don't know, isn't that what you're supposed to be telling me?"

Book knowledge is worthless without experience, in my eyes. I don't learn that way. I can learn that way when integrated with experience, but I don't claim to understand something fully unless I have experienced it myself. I can understand if I have experienced something similar, but even then I wouldn't fully claim to know a thing, only to partially understand.

One thing the counselors did no one else in my life did before was listen. They encourage me to talk, then sat back and listened.

And with this came another revelation. I could tell about my pain, about my abuse, and it was the same as if I didn't tell. Nothing changed. Where were the doctors who could take care of this disease? These people, these doctors of the head didn't test, they didn't diagnose, and they didn't offer any treatment to make me well.

I picture these people standing at the bank counter, cashing their check, and laughing hysterically.

And the biggest crusher of the whole experience, as I finally thought someone would help me, finally thought my parents cared about what I had been through, was everyone blew me off. The counselors blew me off for family issues. My parents blew me off for family issues. They talked about blended families, stepchildren, blah, blah, blah, blah, blah. All these people wanted me to remain mummified.

I am invisible, a ghost.
The space I occupy is felt by not one.
I am a mist that floats through the air,
Unnoticed,
Unobserved,
A droplet falls upon your skin,
You pause for an instant,
Wipe away the inconvenience,
And without a word,
Forget.

15 *the* THERAPIST

This seems like the perfect time to mention my therapist. Our therapist/crazy person relationship lasted for most of the twenty-second year of my life. During that time this man tried to make me hate my dad and other men in my life. I'm not sure how he did this—implications, I think—but I was not weak minded; he wasn't going to mess with my memories.

It's funny, though, while I was seeing him, I was insanely obsessive in a sort of bizarre mind torment. I saw the male organ I earlier referred to as a semi everywhere. Not real ones, but objects that turned into this organ. I would be driving and the car's exhaust pipe in front of me would catch my attention, and as soon as it did, it would become this male tormenting organ. A chunky tree branch would instantly become what I viewed as my cancer-causer. A telephone pole would remind me of this organ, a very large, monstrous, scary one, I might add. A tormenting male organ here, there, they seemed to be everywhere. It was crazy.

I didn't tell my therapist this. I just took my little white slip with my prescription refill written upon it and went my way.

It seems that he, too, could find a way to keep me incapacitated and from messing with my wrappings. Dope her up.

(Note, by the way, when I stopped the drugs, I stopped seeing male organs. This was just my experience and should not be taken to mean anything to anyone else that sees male organs or any other apparition for that matter. I just wanted anyone who knows me and reads this, to know that I have recovered from this and no longer have these "semi sightings.")

~~~~~~~~~~~~~~~~~

Craziness eludes,
Teases,
Taunts,
Terrifies me.

~~~~~~~~~~~~~~~~~

16 *the* FREAKS

Throughout my growing up we moved around a lot. I never had the chance to make lasting childhood friendships; I was always new to a school, a neighborhood. When I finally made some friends with the record of living three years in the same area, my mother found her third husband, Mr. Twizzle, and moved us again. Right smack dab in the middle of dreadful junior high.

By this age the cliques were formed, friendships established. And I felt misplaced; I always felt misplaced. Mr. Twizzle had a boy my age, and my new brother was great. He had charisma, a personality loved by all. He knew music, bands. He played kick-butt drums. He was very cool and had no problem establishing himself in the new school of ours.

And with that, he helped me make friends. And our friends were like us, straight from the cave of dysfunction. We find each other, you know. Maybe it's an energy we exude, or a look in our eyes. Whatever it is, Pain KNOWS Pain. And we want friends who KNOW us. We *find* friends who know us.

When this group was around, people noticed them, they stood out. Dysfunction, deformity, disease, and symptoms everywhere from the wombs of something we call families, parents, older siblings, aunts, uncles, raising their children under alcoholism, drug addiction, being unaware workaholics, beaters, screamers, sexual predators, incest inflictors…

These children of dysfunction couldn't be missed—anyone's childhood formed by such wombs as these, creating all that mutilation now crowding one area. One with no arms, one with a misshaped head, another missing fingers, and a few with toe-misplacement. And only we looked at each other, only *we* belonged to each other, because no one else wanted to look at us or bother with us.

So then, they too, the "normal" ones in their happy little families, tried to get rid of us, the rejects, the freak show, the ones never to be the favorites, never to be encouraged or cheered like those in student council blazers, football uniforms, and letter jackets, or like the ones carrying pom-poms. We, the mutated freaks, never had a chance in the world beyond the tent of the circus.

The rest of the "normals," shut us out of their sight, turned their backs, or sent us away.

Detention was one option, trapped in a room with other mutants, our kind, imprisoned by some teacher who was forced to sit there with us, rarely looking up from the desk.

Some of the time the teachers or staff would get rid of us altogether by sending us home, or forcing us to stay home, banned from the school.

"A free day from the mutants, let their parents be forced to look at them."

But they didn't look at us either. They turned their heads or shut us in our room.

Is my life worth living,
My love worth giving?
The hands answer,
The shoulders reply,
A turn of the head reveals,
I look to the floor.
And I cry.

17 *the* U-HAUL

As an adult, I spent large amounts of time working through the healing process when it came to understanding my childhood, where I came from, what I had gone through. I felt the anger inside of me, and I wasn't sure where it all was coming from.

It seemed as I worked through one situation, overcame one aspect of anger from my childhood, another would come up. They became the small battles I worked through to form a war. These battles continue to this very day, and I am beginning to understand that fighting is a lifetime process.

It is a process we need to embrace; understanding the process brings us closer to healing. Every time we feel we are going backward, when our happiness turns into anger or pain, we are not really going backward at all. We have actually spent a lot of time moving forward to get to the point we can confront another part of us that holds pain, abandonment, distress, unhappiness, confusion, or any other result of pain that may bring negativity, sickness, and disease into our lives. The end of the battle comes, we just can't see the end all of the time.

Sometimes a battle hits me unexpectedly. I can be moving through life just fine, thinking I am on a land that is beautiful and free of enemies and bam! I run into a wall. Usually I fall on my rear because I'm so oblivious to anything going on around me when I'm happy. It's not like I cautiously watch and wait for the next wall. I have hit so many you'd think I would watch, but I don't. Happiness is an emotion that I thrive on and suck in to the last possible drop.

I hit one particular wall in a burger drive-thru line, and it was one that would scan most my childhood.

I was waiting behind a U-haul. The bright orange color of this large truck blurred as I focused in on the shiny silver lever on its locked gate. I could feel the mental bricks beginning to fall around me, blocking me, forcing me to look at them. A scene from the past began to play out in my mind.

I was nine. We were parked at a rest stop along some endless stretch of highway before and beyond us. I had never seen such masses of land, trees, and mountains.

The gate of our rented large orange U-haul was unlocked, the back lifted with a loud rush of metal grinding on metal.

There, in the back, sat my hamster cage. I looked for him, my little hamster. He was hiding in his toilet paper tube.

I had to pick up the tube. Shake him out. His tiny little claws scratching to keep himself hidden.

I held him in my sweating palms and sympathized with him.

He was afraid and in the little movement of his whiskers upon his face, he somehow spoke for me.

He wanted to know where…

Where we were going,

And why? Why was he trapped in this huge truck for hours and days with everything we owned?

I stroked his little body, put him close to my face and tried to be brave for him, reassure him as best my little self could.

I sat down on the curb next to the giant orange truck and replayed what brought me here, to this strange land. Mom said it would be an adventure.

They had just put in the pool, my mother and Trucker Tom, her second husband. As kids, we were excited for the beautiful underground pool in our own backyard—to swim in anytime we wanted.

We watched and waited, anticipated. They dug the hole, poured the cement, put in the liner, and filled it the top with crisp, cool, sparkling water. And then we packed. And we left—in a big orange U-haul. Everything we owned. Everything I owned—my clothes, my stuffed animals, my toys, books, and my hamster.

My vision faded, I paid for my food and threw it to the seat next to me. This was not a wall I wanted to charge into or look at. But there it was, and I wasn't going to get past it, over it, or around it. I needed to take it down, brick by brick. I pulled away from the drive-thru window and parked my car.

I hit my steering wheel as hard as I could, over and over. It hurt my fists.

"She left with the f---ing pool guy. She left Trucker Tom for the guy who built our pool, after he built the pool, and took us all the way across the country…"

Far, far away from everyone who loved us. Funny thing is that my mother should have left Trucker Tom long before that—years of violence inflicted on her, violence inflicted on her child. Years of watching her hair pulled, her face slapped, dishes broken, furniture thrown during violent outbursts of stupid drunkenness by this man who was supposed to love her.

During those Trucker Tom days, I would lie in my bed and call out for my daddy.

The phone never rang.

And the yelling never stopped. She didn't hide it from us either. She let us see it. As if it would stop her violent husband if we children were watching.

It didn't stop him.

True love.

I should have been thrilled about leaving; it wasn't a safe place. But at nine, even an unsafe place is still home, and I was angry at leaving what I knew as home.

My mother stayed with Trucker Tom until they put a pool in our backyard. We children watched the construction in anticipation, excited about it while my mother was secretly romancing, or being romanced by, the guy building it. Mom then let him take our little family away from Trucker Tom's house and our new pool all the way to what I thought was the other side of the world, like eight states away.

I hated her for that. I was violent. The fear and uncertainty overwhelmed this nine-year-old child, yet the little girl who existed that day could say nothing, do nothing. Not until now, as an adult. As if she saved it inside, almost a quarter of a century, for the moment she would be brave enough to act out the anger, have strong enough vocal cords to voice the rage. Now it was time for the little girl to speak, the day she awoke within me, using my grown up adult body and voice, as she screams and bruises her pounding fists on the steering wheel.

This is what a child does—learns, absorbs, feels, as the womb of his or her life forms them. They soak in their surroundings; hide the pain, the anger, until the child is old enough to use the strength and power of the adult body to act out the emotions they were too small and fearful to act out as a child.

And this, a child spends her growing life waiting for. She will subconsciously act out her deep emotions as a grown person, seemingly uncontrollable, like some kind of programmed person. The child, sitting in the depths of the adult body, with some kind of remote, controlling the person she inhabits.

I remember how she controlled me. I recognize the buttons she pushed to cause the uncontrollable action from me that her anger wanted to produce. That crazy anger would cause my fists to pound my head, or would cause my legs to jump from a moving car and run out into traffic and not stop until I fell into a crying clump in some far away field of weeds.

With this being uncontrollable and out of my sane adult hands, something needed to be done. This little girl needed to be talked to, dealt with, reasoned with. My small child and I needed to share with each other. We needed to speak about the pain, the loneliness, the abandonment, and I, as an adult, needed to share with her my hopes and dreams and vision as a grown person. We needed to figure out how we were going to work through her anger, fear, and rebellion, and how we were going to stop fighting each other so we could find a way to accomplish our hopes and dreams, our vision.

Her main goal was to vent, so I made it my main goal to let her do so in the most non-destructive way possible. I faced the U-haul wall, and I let her vent.

~~~~~~~~~~~~~~~~~~~~~~

Who holds my hand to lead the way?
Whose steps should I study,
To stay the path?
I fear getting lost,
So I study you.
I watch you.
And I trust,
You may know where you are going.

~~~~~~~~~~~~~~~~~~~~~~

18 *the* HAUNTED

We went to a Catholic school down south. We weren't Catholic, but the school was convenient, across the street from our house. And this private school, with their plaid and white uniforms and strict rules, had white people in it. The public school culture, Mom thought, would overwhelm us.

Our house was unbelievable; I had never seen one so big. The old wood floors, the front porch, and big yard, and a pool the pool-guy boyfriend had put in. Maybe I *could* be convinced this was some great adventure.

I did make a new friend there. My hamster was dead at this point, so I befriended a spider that lived in my bedroom window, behind the glass. I needed her, Charlotte, my spider. I had always shared a bedroom with my sister until now, until this big house. My mother thought it was great we could have our own rooms. For me, it was scary, not having my sister around. So I talked to Charlotte, chatted with her while she wrapped her food.

I smoked my first cigarette there. Fourth grade. That's where I started smoking.

No one was watching. I killed time by roaming around this new neighborhood, and I saw ghosts. They hung around the neighborhood, streets upon streets of houses, apartment buildings. I was alone with ghosts that did nothing, said nothing. They lived in the house, they hung around the yard. They stood around buildings talking with each other, they taught classes, and they worked in stores.

I was fine being alone, living in my very own dimension apart from the world. In my ten-year-old mentally I made every other person who existed a ghost, and with this, I protected myself. They couldn't get to me because I convinced myself they weren't real. If they were ghosts, even if they tried to touch me, their hands would go straight through me. I kept myself safe this way. I kept my body and my mind safe this way. No one else existed but me and Charlotte. Charlotte wasn't going to hurt me.

We children traveled back and forth between my dad's state and my mom's state, which spanned a whole country, on school vacations. Once we were left in an airport for four hours. Young. No one was watching. Platters could have been filled, but thankfully no one was eating either.

Hurricane Fredrick hit the state of Alabama, must've leaked into the house, tore up Mom's and the pool guy's relationship, and we left with Mom.

Actually, I found out later my dad went to the courts and demanded she bring us home. Pretty aggressive behavior for such a passive man; I know he must have loved his girls.

Mom was forced to come back. The pool guy wouldn't come with her. True love.

Are you listening?
Where are you?
I am deep within my soul,
In the solitude of my soul.
You cannot come here.
You cannot speak to me when I am here,
In the solitude of my soul.
You can't get to me here.
You cannot hurt me here,
In the solitude of my soul.
I will not let you in.
I will never let you in.

19 *the* TRUEST LOVE

My mother may have missed it early on. As I said, my dad is a very devoted man. He may have been with her to this day had my mother stayed married to him.

But she didn't stay. Someone else caught her eye, spoke to her senses, and manipulated her heart.

Trucker Tom, who became my mother's second husband, before she left for the pool guy, sat in his car in front of our house and waited for her. She wasn't hiding anymore from anyone. It was right there, where my dad could stand in the front window and watch her. Watch her open the passenger door, slide into the seat, and give this man a peck on the cheek, a smile. She made no effort to cover her affections for her new boyfriend.

"Where are you going, Mommy?"

Just a little pat on our rears.

"Go in the house with your daddy now; I will be back for you."

And they pulled away.

Away from her children and away from the man who she stood before God with, vowing to love forever.

I don't know if my dad cried. But I know the pain had to have run deep. We were daddy's girls, and he must've known she was going to take us away—away from the security of our home—away from the man who loved us, who would never have shown anything but love and acceptance to us. Away from the truest love who ever existed in my little life. Away, through the gates of hell, to the place where my future tormentor was waiting, into hell itself.

~~~~~~~~~~~~~~~~~~~~~~

Does the heart speak truth,
Or does it deceive?

~~~~~~~~~~~~~~~~~~~~~~

20 *the* ROOTS

The problem was my dad didn't raise his voice, didn't lift a finger against my mother. She was taught that love hurts. And my dad didn't hurt her. The home she shared with my dad became too predictable, too monotonous, and too normal; it wasn't home to her.

God tried to save my mother, gave my dad the stomach to look upon the scars of her soul placed there by her own father. She wasn't comfortable with a love like the faithful, secure, trusting love my dad gave her. So she found someone who would love her like she was trained to be loved. She created for herself a home that was more like the one in which she grew up, filled with mystery and intrigue as to what was going to happen next, constant action. She created for herself a home like her own growing up with the alcoholic, violent, crazy, second husband, Trucker Tom.

Her mother, my grandmother, was an alcoholic, oblivious to the world around her, or so we would like to think. The thought of Grandma knowing what her own husband was doing to his daughter would turn any decent mother's stomach.

My mother's father was a mad drunk, who found it acceptable to take ownership over his flesh and blood, lie upon it, and mix it with his own.

Both sadness and anger run deep into the very center of my bones when I imagine this. While I was discovering my sexual abuse at fifteen, she was still experiencing hers.

I am the third born grandchild on this side of the family, the first girl.

My mother had a child before me, one I didn't grow up with. She was sixteen and loved her boyfriend. They would have gotten married, she said. She wanted him to be her husband, and she wanted that baby to love. She got neither.

The evil man, whom she called her dad, forced her into some kind of seclusion for pregnant teenagers, and made her give away the baby, chased off the one she loved, too, forbidding their beautiful young romance.

The little bit of life that remained in her had just forcefully forfeited a large chunk of itself, never to be gotten back. The womb of the incestuous father and the womb of incredible loss formed her; those cells were put into places they never should have been, doing their job, remembering, placing, fixing, mutating.

And so, a heavy, cement cover named Pain is lifted. A cause is discovered. But there is another Pain and another cause.

The Bible says, in Exodus chapter 34, God does not forget the guilty, visiting the iniquity, the sins, to the third and fourth generations. Somewhere in this family tree this cycle of abuse needed to stop. Somewhere it was destined to stop. Through understanding, healing, wisdom, and will, this family tree of terror needed to be put down, cut from the stump, or pulled from the roots.

And so it goes back. I hated my grandfather. I hated him before I even knew what he did to my mother. I was afraid of him, and I didn't know why.

That baby boy my mother gave up was being protected. Had my mother raised him, my grandfather would have gotten to him.

He got to her sister's son, changed him from a sweet little boy, first born grandson into a mutant. But where were this little boy's wrappings? What was going to hide his scars?

Maybe he chose to wear his own hand-picked mummy wrappings, maybe not, but he found his group. The ones with similar scars, similar mutation, and there he stands with approximately 1 percent of the American population, fighting for their rights to be seen and heard, with their scars. Never to know love on earth the way God intended it to be.

Cursed.

Cursed with the end of the third and fourth generation curse.

The other grandchildren were lucky. Their grandfather died when they were young, and I don't think the perverted beast got even an appetizer out of them. Myself? I am unsure.

Years later I met a woman and discovered there may be a reason this old man called my grandfather scared the hell out of me. A psychic lady came into the bar I worked in on a slow night. I served her the drink she ordered, and we started a conversation. She told me of her so-called gift and began to read me.

I looked around, made sure no one needed me. I propped my elbows onto the bar and placed my face into them with a smile, ready to hear what she had to say.

She pinned my past. My abuse. Even said that she could name my abuser. My first stepbrother's name was in the forefront of my mind, but the name out of her mouth was unrecognizable. Then she told me of the second. I realized days later the first was the name of my dead grandfather. I didn't really care; I was still unsure but it could explain why I hated him.

Should I hate him? Or should I hate his mother? His mother was strange. I remember her as a creepy woman who wore long black dresses and sat in her chair in her huge old mansion and recited scary verses from a bible. She and her husband adopted my grandfather at the age of two, and they had no idea what to do with a child, no instinct or unconditional love for this young boy they were raising. I believe to have such horrid, evil roots of alcoholism and sexual predatory, someone in my grandfather's original family came from the pits of hell. For all I know demons raised him and subjected him to torture his first two years of life, which is unknown to the family. What the family did know was his new parents continued to bring torture as they ordered this little boy to sit in complete silence in a chair for hours, while his parents, who should have been playing with the child they so desperately wanted, entertained, for days on end, other adults.

〜〜〜〜〜〜〜〜

A death leaves a demon homeless.
And so he searches,
Follows the blood path,
Until he finds another,
From the generation beyond,
To take over,
To inhabit,
One that recognizes him,
One that finds him familiar,
One that opens their soul,
Welcomes his destruction.

〜〜〜〜〜〜〜〜

21 *the* MIRROR

Counseling failed to do really anything for me, mental health intervention failed, the church, the therapist, none of them seemed to help. I wasn't anywhere even near a diagnosis, let alone a treatment to make me better. I wasn't going to get better.

I was going to get much, much worse. I needed to get much, much worse. I needed to fall deep into the pits of despair before I found the way and the will to pick myself up and climb out of the bottomless hole that horrid being named Pain tried to trap me in until death reached me.

And with my pain I felt fear. Fear of who I was, who I was going to become, what I was going to do. I carried a haunting fear that I would become my mother.

I drank like her.

I became pregnant as a teenager like her.

Had flings like her.

People said I even looked like her.

I was afraid that when I looked into the mirror, I would see her face, that I would live her life.

Words rang in my head. *How do I break the mirror? How do I break the mirror?* Over and over, again. *My mother, the mirror; how do I break the mirror?* For days I went crazy with these words. I believed I was going crazy. I believed her life and decisions to be crazy, unstable, and impulsive. I never wanted that kind of craziness to be in my own life and decisions.

But I can feel her deep inside of me. I can feel my mother's wants, needs, and desires echoing, calling out to me in the depths of my soul. Wants, needs, and desires that seem irrational, against moral rules and obligations I know to be true and right in the eyes of the people around me.

I see my mother, and all at once, while I admire her strength and independence, I also hate her for it. I hate what it has taught me, but at the same time, knowing it is a part of me, knowing if I am to succeed within myself, I must embrace the strength and independence I spent so much time observing and taking for my own.

Success, freedom, and healing come from deep love and acceptance of self, embracing the good *and bad*. It pays well to seek wisdom regarding our make up. Searching the depths of who we are, who we came from, and who we've become can bring understanding to fears that haunt us, fears that cripple and paralyze us.

Fear comes in two forms, real or imagined. Both have the ability to accomplish their purpose. Real fear can protect you, keep you from danger. When you stand before a raging dog, his yellowed teeth exposed, saliva streaming from his lips, fear tells you to get away, fast. With that, your real fear has accomplished safety.

The second form is imagined fear. This fear can paralyze you, keep you from living, or, with confrontation, accomplish new goals. Once you have chosen to identify and embrace this imagined fear, it can cause you to achieve.

My mother's strength, independence, bravery, and rebellion scared the hell out me. It was a door I was fearful about opening. The results of her most inherent qualities made me very afraid of accessing the same qualities within me. I feared the very same results—divorce, instability, lack of love, alcoholism, aloneness. I feared to the very root of *my self* what I viewed to be the result these qualities wrought in *her* life.

The negative outcome exists when I stand before that dreaded door and my fear keeps me from opening it.

Negative, because I have come to realize the qualities I need in my life to reach healing, purpose, and destiny are contained within that very room I am so fearful of entering. What I desperately need to confront my pain, my fears, and my insecurities, are held within those very qualities my mother displayed—strength, independence, courage. *My fear keeps me from the very qualities I need to access if I want to confront my fear.*

I confused this sort of fear with real fear. Real fear that tells me to run, thus accomplishing safety. This imagined fear also told me to run, thus accomplishing safety, but that was wrong because I only saw one kind of result from possessing these inherent qualities my mother held—negative conclusions in life—alcoholism, divorce, adultery, aloneness, depression. My fear distorted my impression of her, of her qualities. I thought that to keep from having negative results in my own life, these qualities similar in me needed to be inactive, run from, and pushed away.

It took time to understand it is not the qualities that produce the results; it is what you *do* with the qualities. I need not to fear these qualities, but embrace them to live. The very same water that fills the lungs and causes death also sustains life. It is not about the water or the fault of the water; it is what you are *doing with* the water—drinking or drowning.

~~~~~~~~~~~~~~~~~~~~~~~~~~~~~~~~

Tell me, Mother,
Why am I so afraid of you?
Who you are,
Who you've become?
When will I get away?
And be who I am supposed to be?
By bearing me have you brought a curse?
Or with understanding,
Have I been blessed beyond belief?
Will you have produced a life,
That takes a curse intended,
And breathes life,
Passes on wisdom,
And hope,
To the generations beyond?
Tell me.

~~~~~~~~~~~~~~~~~~~~~~~~~~~~~~~~

22 *the* BOUNDARIES

My parents during my adolescence, my mother and Mr. Twizzle, had the strictest of rules at home. Minor offenses caused strict laws to be passed, five minutes after curfew, a forgotten check-in. Stupid things like that. There was no mercy. No room to grow.

The impersonal boundaries such as when I had to be home, what was allowed as far as outside activities, and the results expected as far as behavior and acceptable grades in school were set in stone. Those expectations and consequences were very clear—if you did this, then you get that—and very important to a child, important to keep life clear, understood, and safe.

The personal boundaries were not so clear, and overlooking a boundary of any sort, a child or adolescent becomes very afraid, panicked, and unsure.

Childhood sexual abuse eliminates the inherent knowledge of a boundary. At first, the boundary is there, I believe, for most of us. If there weren't an inherent knowledge of this personal boundary, then such shame and guilt wouldn't come from the invasion of it. Absence of shame and guilt when penetrating a boundary or having a boundary invaded tells me those boundaries had never been established, thus causing a warped sort of view when it comes to acts that are acceptable or not acceptable. Sometimes those boundaries are later established, and sometimes never. Possibly, sexual intimidators don't understand, or never understood, the idea of personal boundaries.

As a simple note, I want to add that any form of sexual intimidation qualifies for abuse. Any intimidation through words or actions is a form of abuse and invasion of boundary. Words over toned in sexual innuendo or suggestion. Actions such as exposing private parts, making sexual hand movements. Sexual intimidation can make a person or child intimidated, shameful, or afraid without even being touched.

As a small child, I was never empowered when it came to protecting my personal boundaries. I learned to view myself as "an object for the taking." As a child I was at the mercy of the adult instruction around me, and this I carried, to the point of what I call my "prison break."

Only as a young adult, did I somewhat come to understand my choice of freedom in whose nude body I wanted to look at or who I would allow to touch me in certain places, in certain ways. I say somewhat, because in a sense, my striving to produce choice in the matters of nudity and touching also imprisoned me. This would later produce promiscuity.

My constant need to have control over my choice of sexual partners and acts brought promiscuity to my life. I felt I was safe from the shame and guilt as long as I was choosing to perform a sexual act and not having it imposed on me against my will. In some sort of warped way of thinking, I took sex willingly at every opportunity as not to leave any room for unwanted, undesired advances, ever. I even turned a date rape around in my mind to produce the façade of a willing act to protect myself from the shame.

But this so-called protection fought against me, too. Along with the shame of past abuse, sex with anybody and everybody

ate me up, gave away another piece of my very precious, intimate
self to people who were nothing more than just sexual partners to
prove I was somehow living with sexual choice.

～～～～～～～～～～～

How is it your gaze can peer right through me?
Why is it your hands so large can get to me?
I wake and choose my dress,
How I wish it were made of metal,
With chains and locks that have no key,
Not seen through,
Not easily torn away.

～～～～～～～～～～～

23 *the* BREAK

I met my "*Grease 2 guy*" at the beach the summer before I turned seventeen. I had been obsessed with the movie that year, so when I saw this guy I connected him with the movie and let him talk to me. We started to meet at the beach regularly, and eventually we started a relationship.

My mother and Mr. Twizzle didn't like my older boyfriend, or should I say, they didn't like his age. I was sixteen and he was twenty-two. They forbade me to date him. So I had to sneak around to see him. Sleep all day and sneak out with him at night. One would think they, especially my mother, would have known teenage love.

He and I would have been better monitored beneath their own roof, maybe during the day when they could have kept tabs on our whole relationship. It would have been wise for them to know a couple will find a way, and a place, to be together if they so choose.

Tabs weren't kept and this relationship wasn't monitored. By their definition, it shouldn't have existed, period. So, it existed behind their backs, and any future defining was left to me. The door was closed, and I would get no advice or help from my parents.

Oh, how we need to see a gentle, guiding hand does so much more than incessant, prison guard-type force. A soft, nudge in the right direction feels safe, full of care and concern. Harsh, rigid judgment and rules feel cold, empty, and make me want to rebel.

～～～～～～～～～～～

The glare upon the metal hurts my eyes,
The chill upon the metal startles my palms,
The strength of the metal confines me.
You stand on the outside looking in,
Why won't you open the door?
Why won't you set me free?

～～～～～～～～～～～

24 *the* NEIGHBORHOOD

We moved in together, this "*Grease 2* boyfriend" and I. We lived in a run down, uncared for, icky neighborhood, one very unpleasing to the eye. Dead grass; paint flaking on houses; yards and streets littered with garbage; and mean, nasty dogs with glared teeth, saliva hanging from their jowls, tied up to metal fences.

Scar bearers live in places like this. An area they designate just for them. With streets placed just so, so the normal citizen will not have to drive by and see the places the mutants gather, the hell holes in which they reside. These neighborhoods lie tucked away in one corner or another, freeways and passageways placed just so these neighborhoods can be passed over and forgotten about.

People stay up all night in these neighborhoods. They wait for the dark. And then come out of their caves. It seems evil likes the darkness in which to hide its ugly self and the people he inhabits.

Here is how evil presented himself. The sun set and darkness covered the dimly lit streets, his indication to prepare the stage. First, he pulled out his props and created his atmosphere.

The booze bottles were opened and emptied. Then bags of pot were smoked, pills were popped. In a matter of minutes the effects of these props began to fill the people, overtake them, and completely transform anyone willing to be subject to evil's little game in their life. People's faces physically started to change. Their speech became lazy, slurred, and filled with obscenities. Every sense they possessed became dulled, so evil could perform his masteries.

As soon as the atmosphere was blanketed with the blackest of darkness, evil took center stage.

His co-actors—Hatred, Resentment, Anger, Revenge—were all there to perform their show.

And what a show it was.

If you wanted to have the hell scared out of you.

Someone rammed a fist through the wall or a shoulder through a door, bloodied themselves or someone around them, screamed, hit, bit. This was no horror movie playing flatly on a screen. This was a live performance, and audience members became more than observers, they became participants as well.

Words were shouted that should never be heard, ever, by anyone. People were spitting and devilish laughter would break out at the tears of the intimidated. Fist fights, knife throwing, scratches, cuts, broken noses, and more blood were produced until only one participant remained standing, until only one held the power in the room. Then the curtain would close. Quiet would enter, and a nervous peace would come once more. Until tomorrow, when it would all begin again.

My mother visited me there once. She stood in my bedroom facing the mattress that held the ghostly image of her seventeen-year-old daughter sleeping in that very spot with this man her daughter was living with, this man my mother abhorred.

My mother stood there, somehow calling out to me. Her face wasn't, nor her words, but I know somehow her heart was calling. She just didn't know how to do it, how to talk to me. So I punished her. I stood across the room from her with my arms crossed and told her I was fine, and I was happy living where I was.

I, too, was calling out to her. Not my face, nor my words, but my heart. As I told her I was okay, tears began to drop. I left with her that day. But she didn't take me home. She said I needed help. *Why couldn't she help me?* I wondered. All I needed was a mother, one who cared, wanted to direct me as I needed to be directed. She said she could do nothing for me; she didn't know what to do with me. So she took me to the hospital—the mental health unit and I checked myself in.

For the moment I thought the unit to be a welcome retreat from all the craziness in my life. I thought I finally landed somewhere I could get some help from all the turmoil going round about in my head. I knew I wasn't a normal person. I knew it wasn't normal to want to slaughter myself all of the time. I knew I needed someone to do something; I knew I needed help.

But the hospital wasn't quite what I expected. It was more like a jail. It was all about routines: groups, one-on-one therapy schedules, wake up times, bed times, eating schedules. It didn't take me very long to figure out this wasn't the place for me. I lay in my bed in my little room and looked out my little window, and I laughed to myself, what a joke! I had just checked myself into a prison. I checked myself out the next evening.

As an adult today, I know the one thing I really needed at sixteen. I wasn't mentally ill, I was confused, depressed. All my actions were a symptom to a disease no one could reach, especially a stranger. My mother passed me on to family counselors, school counselors, this hospital, and in her final frustration, emancipated me shortly after I checked myself out and went back to my boyfriend. We rarely spoke after that day.

What I needed was my mother. I desperately wanted my mother to talk with me about life, about experiences, about mysteries. I'm not sure why she was so afraid to talk to me, or why any mother is afraid to talk to her daughter for that matter. But the mother is the one closest to her daughter. Shouldn't she try to teach, direct, listen, and be a support for this young woman she is raising? At all costs? With understanding, grace, and mercy?

Depending on how early communication is established determines how wide the chasm is between parent and child. I now include sons and fathers in this topic. We know by the time we are adolescent if the door to a parent's heart is open to discuss concerns, difficulties, dilemmas, etc. We have tested these waters as children, and these waters our children test themselves. If we, as parents, pull them under and scare them with our reaction, our children may steer clear from us as reactor and the chasm may grow.

We need to pluck confusion from adolescents who are merely just years from adulthood and being on their own. We need open communication, not close-mindedness or ignorance, between parents and their children when it comes to sex (with others or with themselves), disease, drugs, drinking, fear, faith, and so on, especially when we are fighting cable television program's portrayals of sex and drinking through dating shows and such. I have yet to see on these networks a follow-up with the gynecologist telling the young girl who is getting drunk, showing her cleavage, and giving sex freely, that she now has bugs crawling all over her privates.

～～～～～～～～～

Where does life hide?
Where does she conceal herself?
How can I find her in this childish game,
Of hide and seek?
Why does she hide so well?
Why can't I hear her breathe?
Her heart beat?
How is it she hides so well?

～～～～～～～～～

25 *the* BABY

My mother said that she knew as I sat before her, said she noticed that my jeans weren't buttoned.

My body had changed and my young teenage figure was fading. What would normally be a pleasurable sight for a grown, married woman expecting to manifest a sign of the love and commitment between her and her husband was repulsively sad for me as a young girl.

I was seventeen, still in high school, adding another obvious sign to my mutant state. I delivered my baby girl three weeks before my eighteenth birthday, seven days after I completed high school early.

Two months later, we had our graduation practice on the football field. I brought my baby with me, in her stroller. She looked cute, her clean baby hair blowing in the soft wind, a brand new pink dress on. It was one of the first times her dad allowed me to take her out of the house—he was over protective and wouldn't even allow me to take her out of her pajamas, let alone take her out of the house.

Anyway, while on the school football field this little blonde woman approached. (One of those *adults*, you remember.) A teacher from a class I never took and didn't know. She was coming for me, and she was carrying an invisible sword. Her steps landed heavy, pounding against the earth she walked on.

She lifted her sword as she came close, flaunted it, lifted it higher, then plunged.

"I hope you don't think that you are bringing *that* baby to graduation."

Her words shocked the "proud little mama joy" out of me. For the very first time I felt shame—shame for myself, shame for my baby. And shame drove its dagger deep, deep into my heart and soul.

Take your eyes off of my baby, witch! Of course, I'm not going to bring her! What do you think I am? Stupid?

I hung my head low and said quickly and quietly, "No, ma'am."

I felt judgment, very swift, cruel judgment from such a sweet looking woman. I imagined her beautiful, made up, smooth-skinned mask, blonde wig, and costume ripped away to reveal the ugliest, wartiest witch anyone could ever imagine seeing.

I wished I had known a little more about judgment back then—that it was *her* issue; she had a problem with an unwed teenage mother feeling proud of her baby. Had I known at the time the sentence from her mouth was about her own insecurities or self-viewed failures in life, I wouldn't have been haunted with the shame of being a teenage mother.

But the thing is we are taught "adults know." We are taught to look up to them, aspire to them, but we're not taught all should not be aspired to. Many adults we grow up around are shallow, with unresolved issues they fill the world with as they come in contact with other people daily. Their judgments, and unresolved issues of rejection and such, are invisible poisons they pass into the atmosphere every time they breathe or use their voice.

There are many other ways that insecure blonde could have

approached me to ensure I wouldn't be carrying my baby through the commencement line. Had she instead carried compassion and understanding and love, had she approached with a bouquet of flowers and not a sword, she could have achieved the same necessary result, and not poisoned another person whose path she crossed, giving Pain even more power to open the door to Death.

Did this deceivingly beautiful blonde witch have any idea her swift judgment and choice of words furthered my fantasies of suicide? Of course not, she is the type of person only concerned with herself and her power over a young girl. Did she care her placement of guilt and shame within me only fed my pain? Doubtful. I can explain my feelings like this.

When Pain already occupies your soul, becomes a part of you, when he lives within you, there will be moments of reprieve, moments when Pain is weak and tired and thus not very active within. Then, as suddenly as a quick slice of a knife, Pain awakens and his voice heard clear.

Shame, guilt, and intimidation feed Pain. These three things nourish him and give him strength within the body he inhabits, strength to rise up and invite his co-conspirator, Death, in for a visit. This woman walked up with a small feast for the pain that resided in my soul. She fed him, and she paved a portion of the path within me to help Death find his way.

Pain cannot destroy us if we understand this process and refuse to accept the food others offer our Pain. We can say, "No, that may be your choice of nourishment, but it is not mine. Keep it to yourself; I want no part of your meal."

In essence, when we realize we don't need to accept these things from others, we are refusing judgment and negativity. When a nasty comment comes our way, we can hold up our shield and say, "*Your* bitterness, your hate, your rejection are *your* issues. They have nothing to do with me, who I am, my character, or my choices."

The rejecter's issues! The one filled with hate or bitterness, *it is all about them*. They only attack us because of what they need to hide in themselves. A dirty look, a stab, a jeer, it's all about *their* insecurities, *their* sadness, *their* hopelessness. We need to carry our umbrellas high to keep their poison from falling upon us, and with that, we will keep our Pain at bay.

And if by chance a drop of poison falls on you, don't just sit and cry, or whine about its unbearable sting. **Wipe it away, forget about it.** It is *their* poison, not yours.

～～～～～～～～～

I am free from you,
Your words, your looks,
Your poison spittle,
Will not rest upon my head.
And thus, you shall wither,
For your job will not be accomplished,
You shall wither as the grass,
Beneath a blazing hot sun,
My freedom brazen,
Burning you,
Your evil glare,
And your very words.

～～～～～～～～～

26 *the* QUALITIES

My mother was beautiful. I have a picture of her standing in the kitchen, her little baby girl sitting in a high chair. Her long, black, perfectly-placed hair held off of her soft complected, elegantly made face with a thick, dark headband. And her great outfit, classy, very in-style with the times, short skirt and long, black, heeled boots covering her thighs.

She wasn't posing for a picture. It was a moment snatched out of the fleeting of time. Some small twinkling of opportunity seized by, maybe my dad, for a monument to my mother, of her motherhood, a moment otherwise lost forever.

In my picture, she was feeding me, giving love and care, keeping her young child alive. At least I owned one picture representing her love, her giving of herself to the little one who came from her.

My mother is an amazing woman, very smart, the kind of woman who turned people's heads—the kind who said, "I don't care about myself, and so, I will care about you."

No one likes to be in the presence of someone who can't stop talking about themselves, about who they are, or what they've done. After a while listeners get completely bored.

Most everyone wants to be seen and heard, waiting for the opportunity to open up and share.

Most everyone.

Some don't.

Some don't want to share; some just want to listen. For some, sharing would be bringing the pain up to the surface. So they don't share. They listen. They just care about you, and they won't share, especially if they are not asked.

I imagine my mother this way: smart, friendly, fun, concerned for those around her—doing everything possible to keep her pain parked, locked in its self-given box.

I imagine her dreams, her hopes. She could have been a very powerful woman, had she not spent so much time hiding her pain.

She was a treasure to behold. Her beauty. Her care and concern for others. Her sweet voice. Her polite words carefully picked from the heart of one who, having been injured, didn't want to injure.

She drew attention, quite possibly while not wanting it.

There aren't many women out there who can attract men like she could, and I don't believe it is all about beauty. There are many so-called beautiful women who are repulsive to be around.

And so men, who understand this, will do what they can to get the attention of this other sort of woman, the one less concerned for herself, the one who will care for him.

They hunt the treasure and sift at the creek side. Day after day, month after month, they search. They search, and they pass over many women who have yet again turned out to be "fool's gold."

My mother wasn't "fools gold." She was the real thing, and when they met her, they knew it.

Smart. Not to be misunderstood for book intelligence, but the kind they call "street smart," a person who has life experience and has the wisdom to observe, to analyze, and draw from life experience.

A person with life experience can "see through" that which is presented before her and have deep knowing and revelation within her heart and mind.

My mother was this sort of person. She stood out.

But she didn't want to stand out anymore. She wanted to keep temptation far from her.

So she gained weight. Made herself fat, tried to look like "fools gold" and be passed over by men. Keep them from wanting her.

It didn't help.

Being her draw wasn't about outer beauty, changing her form didn't make her repulsive. It might have helped, but it didn't solve the problem altogether.

My mother was a magical person inside and as long as she was alive and not agoraphobic, she wouldn't be able to hide her magic. For even if she was agoraphobic, eventually the furnace would have to be fixed, or the stove replaced, eventually she would have to speak to a treasure hunting man, and he wouldn't help but be drawn by her sparkle.

And the fat? It did what fat does. It depressed her.

She no longer looked in the mirror and saw the amazing woman she had become, the part of her that she was proud of. She saw a protrusion of skin, a warped, contorted version of herself, an explosion of the mask, covering up the things she thought she needed to hide.

And when she looked in the mirror she saw the mask.

It reminded her she was covered. It reminded her *why* she was covered. Every single visit in the mirror became a subconscious conversation with Pain.

This was another result, a desperate grasp for control, for a victim feeling loss of control through sexual abuse. Not unlike myself, consciously making myself appealing to attract sex to feel in control, my mother consciously made herself unappealing to ward off sex to feel in control. We choose our own defenses, usually to our detriment, but always out of the need to be in control.

A woman and her little girl wander upon,
Two flowers, standing side by side,
One tall, prominent, bright, lovely in color.
Loved.
The other sad, faded, brown around the edges,
Dismissed.
The woman bends and picks the flower of prominence.
The little girl's heart asks,
Why does the eye always love?
And why does the eye always dismiss?

27 *the* WORDS

At seventeen, I was becoming an adult, fast—learning to cook the meals, do the dishes, do the laundry, clean the house, and mother a baby. I was oblivious to doing these things a short time before. This was obvious to any onlooker, as I proudly thought the dishes were done, overlooking the crusty pans sitting on the dirty stove. My ignorance in plain sight as I stood and blankly eye-balled the splattering bacon and wondered if I had to flip this stuff. I had no idea what I was in for, with all these chores around me.

I belonged out there somewhere where the rest of my peers were—the mall, the movies, the hangouts. But I wasn't out there. I was stuck inside, working, starting a family. Too young.

My friends were at the beach, playing, laughing, and experiencing "normal" life.

Not like I was, like I should have been. Experiencing life my way was depressing. My *Grease 2* boyfriend had too much time on his hands, and he used it to criticize every little thing I did or said. Nothing about me could make this guy happy.

"You're a fat, ugly slob."

He demeaned me daily.

I looked in the mirror. I *was* fat and ugly. I cried.

"Mental case." His label for my despair and tears.

He made me feel I could have controlled what was happening to my body, my mind, my emotions. It confused me even more. At the time, I didn't understand that what was happening inside of me came from uncontrollable circumstances I experienced on the *outside* of me. I didn't see the battle with Pain, I didn't see the planned conquest by Death. I began to further hate who I was, who I had become.

And so, I went to my closet. I looked upon that tiffany cloth lying in a clump. I picked it up, shook off the dust, dried my tears, hardened my heart, and slowly mummy-wrapped my scars once again.

I did not understand who I was or who I was to become on the inside was a separate entity from what and who was on the outside. I confused the weapons my enemies used against me to be about me and for me. If the weapons were coming at me, I somehow deserved them.

How is it we let people define our very selves? Why would we give just anyone the authority to tell us who we are? These, who would choose to define the lives of others, are imperfect creatures themselves. They have pasts, secrets, and agendas. Especially agendas. And these agendas are only there to further their own selves.

There are an incredible number of people out there in the world waiting to slaughter you in order to feed their own agendas, usually ones that include power and control.

Everyone has a deep need to feel in control. Some people warp this by using negative, hurtful ways to experience this feeling of being in control. They have learned power is the highway to get to the city, Control and Intimidation, the vehicle they drive to travel there. There is one problem with this vehicle. It comes fully equipped with dirty race car sort of paraphernalia. It is a race car with steel, tire-popping, jagged blades coming out the sides, and a smoker coming out the rear that blinds all other vehicles. This driver is only concerned with his own sight, with his own agenda in reaching his destination. He doesn't care about the destruction and death he leaves in his path. Once he reaches his city, he may look back and apologize, and feel remorse, but, back on that highway he will make the same decisions he did before. How does he get that way and why isn't anyone able to stop him?

~~~~~~~~~~~~~~~~~

I stop along my path and build my bouquet.
Picking pieces that appeal to me,
From here or there.
But somewhere along the line,
My vision has changed,
I look down to find I'm holding,
Dusty, dried up weeds.
I drop them to my feet,
Brush their presence from my palms.

~~~~~~~~~~~~~~~~~

28 *the* POWER

My baby's father was gone most of the time. I took care of our baby. I took her for walks in her stroller. A large amount of my time I spent alone, sad, and depressed, *Grease 2* boyfriend's words ringing in my ears, my self esteem slaughtered by his brainwashing comments of me being crazy and worthless.

I felt worthless to him and to the world.

I believed the things he told me. I believed my baby's father when he said that he loved me. I abandoned my parents, my whole family to be with him, move in with him, to have his child, and then he told me I was absolutely worthless in his sight.

The intimidator has learned about power gained by intimidation. He has seen a father over-power a mother, or a mother a child, or has been intimidated himself.

When a child sees someone put down with intimidation through physical, sexual, or emotional abuse, guilt, or shame, and what it accomplishes, a future intimidator learns to gain his power and control by using such methods of abuse and shame, and the future intimidated learns it is acceptable to be intimidated in such ways. Quite opposite from the rare child who grows to expect his desired results to occur out of love, care, and concern.

This learned intimidation is hard to stop; it is inside and uncontrollable—very, very difficult to overcome. The power-seeker may even be sorry for what he has done or said, but as hard as he tries to stop, his power-seeking drive causes him to once again ridicule, demean, intimidate. The intimidated also reacts to the intimidation, possibly with anger or sadness at the lack of control they suffer. But out of need, necessity, or just familiarity of growing up in "lack of control," the intimidated stay, forgive, and allow themselves to be a target once again.

The process of the intimidator overcome with remorse, and the intimidated with a background of familiarity in being intimidated, creates the "battered person's cycle," and is the reason a woman (or a man), intimidated, can believe their abuser *is* truly sorry for what he has done. She sees it in his eyes, hears it in his voice. It may remind her of a loving parent with bouts of intimidating behavior, possibly the only love she knew was having her physical needs cared for—a home, food on the table, bills paid, etc.—but the emotional needs were neglected. She truly has no idea the emotional needs and nurturing matter just as much as her physical needs. She doesn't understand why it hurts, it just hurts. And being hurt herself, she understands the pain and doesn't want to see him hurt, so she forgives, and forgives again, believing he may change.

There is a problem in this. Chances are he won't change. Chances are, he will soon feel powerless again and will need a victim to regain his power, one who is his closest target, one who is his easiest access. Intimidation will be his weapon of choice. If you're close, if he has access to you, it will be you he uses to gain his power. And again, he will be sorry.

Once you realize you are not going anywhere with this, if you feel your life stifled, and carry a deep desire to move beyond the "battered person's cycle," *you can claim your own power and use your power.* Use it to get free, as free as you can. Run far and fast and do everything you can to eliminate this person's access to you. You cannot be intimidated and used if you cut off all possible contact with this intimidator.

Now, I want to touch on "imagined" intimidation. We've explored real and imagined fear, and as with everything in life there is a psuedo opposite, so I want to explore this with intimidation. Real intimidation brings real harm to our bodies and emotions, and we need to separate ourselves as if a salivating, raging dog were about to eat us, but, with that, we have the confusion of imagined intimidation. And, as with imagined fear, there is nothing real to harm us, just a false feeling that keeps us from accomplishing.

The same analysis applies: imagined intimidation, as with imagined fear, keeps us from the very qualities we need to be whole, feel purpose, and accomplish destiny. Whenever I felt intimidated by the world, I would mummy wrap myself and hide. I was intimidated by whom? The world? I only imagined the world was intimidating me as I sat in tears, paralyzed over some kind of imagined injustice against me. The world wasn't keeping me wrapped. I was. And with that, I was in control, in power. But my power and control were keeping me from every-thing—happiness and the ability to accomplish. I needed to be unraveled and out in "the world" so that my wounds would have air to heal to be whole. I needed to heal to feel purpose, and to accomplish my destiny.

Some other examples of imagined intimidation I have come across are people who won't pick up the phone and make a call to a stranger, someone who won't go into their boss's office and ask for a raise, another who won't stand up against an injus-tice placed upon them, and another completely paralyzed at the thought of addressing a group at a conference.

How is it we are intimidated by a stranger who has never heard our voice or seen our face? Or a boss who hasn't blatantly told us we are a loser undeserving of compensation for our work? Or how is it we think we are small and deserve to suck up an injustice done to us, only to make us look and feel smaller? And how is it we believe a room full of people will stand in judgment of us, what we look like, what we wear, how we sound? We are intimidated by a feeling, *our feelings*, not a person. Identify this enemy and conquer it.

⌇⌇⌇⌇⌇⌇⌇⌇⌇⌇⌇⌇

Two people,
Fighting to be the ruler,
Of one castle.
One with a sword raging,
Raging, swinging.
The other with a shield,
Protecting,
Protecting the bleeding heart.

⌇⌇⌇⌇⌇⌇⌇⌇⌇⌇⌇⌇

29 *the* LOSS

Grease 2 boyfriend's truth slaughtered my self esteem; it came down like a hammer from the sky. Slam, slam, slam. Until I felt so low I had no identity, nothing to give. I became a tiny little speck in a big overwhelming world. My hopes were even smaller.

But someone noticed. This man must've been using a magnifying glass. He found me and made me feel I did have something to give—at least to him.

He knew what to say. He knew how to lift me from my lowered state of rejection. It felt good, and I let him into my life. I loved being around him. I knew when he was with me, he wasn't where he belonged.

I wasn't where I belonged. I didn't care. At home, with my child and her father, I lived in complete torment and rejection. With this other man I floated into a welcoming, but deceiving, abyss.

Then all hell broke loose. I was retreating from our little family we had formed, and this *Grease 2* guy wasn't going to have any of it.

I was completely desensitized by that point. I fought when I cared. But I no longer cared so I no longer fought. And it drove my daughter's father to madness.

He tried everything he could think of. He tried to sweet talk me, utter fond words, and write love letters filled with pleas. But it was too late. I suffered too much ridicule, too much mocking, and too much deriding and taunting from this *Grease 2* guy, from the same mouth he used to confess his love for me.

My heart disconnected.

So he used force as his last attempt—slapping, grabbing, throwing, and strangulation.

He hated me, bloodied me, bruised me, then tried to lie about it.

"No, sir, I didn't lay a hand on her."

It wasn't going to pass. He slapped me so hard and loud across the face both the policemen heard it from outside of the house, from the yard. Imagine a slap so loud it could be heard through walls. Someone finally witnesses a piece of my pain.

A woman's shelter offered my only protection at the time, a welcome retreat, and a chance to get away from this raging maniac. But he planned a different sort of revenge, one that kept his hands from me physically, but where he really used his power was not on my body, but in my head. He chose a place where my injuries were not visible, at least not to anyone who could help.

And he began to plot against me.

Covert action became his biggest claim to fame at the time—the spy, the detective.

He created journals upon journals filled with my every move, my every action—where I went, who I saw, what I did.

He was on a mission. And he was going to take away the little girl, our daughter. He was determined no one else would have her, even if it meant he and his daughter would die together. Come hell or high water, he was going to get her.

Notebooks. Filled. Page after page.

And tapes. Tapes he said were taken from phone conversations and in-person meetings, always trying to get me to say the wrong thing, or the right thing, in his case. And pictures. He would scatter garbage around my bathroom floor and set my daughter in the midst, give her a plugged-in curling iron to hold and snap pictures.

His threats were arrows that weakened my will, my hope. And once he felt the weapons of intimidation working, stealing my power and resolve, the energy went to him. It fueled *his* power and resolve to conquer with intimidation. When he was finished with me, he went after anyone who knew me, trying to get them to speak against me.

The journals, the tapes, and the intimidation set a fear in me so deep I let him take my daughter. I gave up. I gave up my right to be a full-time mother and fought for my self worth ever since.

Predators stalk the fields of our lives,
With mission.
Hiding amongst the thick, dry weeds.
Watching,
Waiting for the opportunity,
To set their teeth,
Into the neck of their prey.

30 *the* DECEPTION

It wasn't until years later that I learned that there was crap in those notebooks. Not enough for a father to get custody. Not even close. I was young, vulnerable, and intimidated, trained to give up my power to anyone who wanted to take it.

The tapes were empty and his pictures would have been worthless before a judge.

I feared this man's intimidation. At this point the real intimidation he put on me when we lived in the same house, causing real fear through physical and emotional battering, had transferred over to intimidation that caused imagined fear, now that we were no longer subject to day-to-day interaction. With him on the outside, he was no longer the salivating, raging dog I was trapped by within four walls, but at the time I had no revelation on the difference.

With imagined fear I gave him power over my life. There were options I could have had, could have taken, could have given myself. But I didn't. I let him dictate to me what was right and wrong with how I lived my life, and with that came slaughtering blows to my self worth.

I shouldn't have kept so much secret. I shouldn't have protected him. I should have shouted from the rooftops what he was doing to me, what he was saying to me. Had I recognized his lies in his now pseudo intimidation, had I realized the truth about myself (that I was a strong and capable mother), had I known truth doesn't come from the mouth of a man who despises me, I could have taken his power.

His intimidation really couldn't harm me. Yet out of this false intimidation came imagined fear—fear that wasn't keeping me from harm, but keeping me from living. I gave this man the power to dictate my life, to tell me what was right and wrong far beyond the time we spent as boyfriend and girlfriend, far beyond our time as united parents.

I let *him* form my perspective on my life. Because he found what he judged to be fault in something I did or said, I let his judgment define me. I also let it bring years upon years of hiding, self hatred, and suicidal torment.

Recently, I learned to shut out these people, the ones who torment me, who judge me, who bring me down, out of my life. And with that learning, I gained freedom, freedom from voices that bring tears, from voices that bring frustration. Now I'm holding the power, the will, and the decision, to fill my ears only with the positive voices I want to hear.

We need to find our life on our own. We need to seek deep to discover who we are from the One who created us. We need to be aware that lies about ourselves will come in other voices, lying voices. Even voices of those supposedly put here to love us. Don't sit in self pity and say, "He is right; I'm worthless, useless, and better off in the gutter." The dialogue in your head needs to be quite the opposite if you plan to conquer and reach your destiny. Pity is a playground and fun for a while, but stay beyond your time and your head will be spinning in confusion. Create your own phrases for yourself, ones that bring confidence and ability and life.

Repeat until you believe, "I am important, I have value and purpose. My destiny is on the horizon!"

I have shut the door to your words,
You have no key.
You won't get in,
You'll never get in.
Turn around,
And go your way,
Far, far,
From my ears,
My eyes,
My thoughts.

31 *the* HOMELAND

I did feel that I had finally been set free in a sense. Contrary to what I wanted to believe, a baby is very overwhelming for a teenager and absent from the daily activities of raising a child, I experienced life a little more like I was supposed to.

I loved my daughter and I cherished every moment I could be with her, but devoid of that day-after-day responsibility is where I really felt free.

Maybe I never was meant to be tied down like a fixed tent. I was comfortable when I could move around, be free to do anything I wanted to on a whim. Like my mother.

It seems that in whatever situation we were raised, whether a good experience or bad, we feel most comfortable within that situation.

I suppose this is why many of us recreate our childhoods in adulthood—because whether good or bad, our memories are what we know, where we feel at home.

A spoiled child often has a difficult time practicing self discipline in adulthood. He is used to getting what he wants, when he wants it. This is home sweet home.

An abused child, or one grown in dysfunction, will feel most comfortable resting his roots in dysfunction, for this is his familiar home.

In either case, anything else feels like foreign soil and, even if a person stays, no matter how long he stays, his soul will long for his war ridden homeland. He will somehow create for himself his war ridden homeland.

When I was hanging out with my peers, living life more like a nineteen-year-old should, I met a guy. He was blonde, with soft, blue eyes, big hands, breathtaking smile, great teeth, massive legs with their hairs placed just so, they made me salivate. The hair, all the way up into his... (There's my hairy butt thing again.)

I fell head over heals for this guy. Maybe I could have married him. I was so in love with him, for a while.

His ambition at the time was to be a trucker. (Just like my mother's awful second husband, Trucker Tom.) "Trucker Tom wanna-be" planned to travel the country on runs and come home in between.

"Wanna-be" wanted to build me a house to keep me home, waiting for him. He said we could sleep with other people when we wanted but would make room for each other when he came back. That was not the fairytale life I had dreamed about.

And when he was around, he really started to treat me like crap.

"Give me a f---ing b--- job or get out of the car."

Oh, God, is he serious or just messing around?

"Give me a f---ing b--- job or I'm kicking you out of the car."

He stops the car, looks into my eyes.

He *was* serious.

"I want a f---ing b--- job. Now!"

Who did he think I was, some street walker he had picked up in the alley? Yah right, I had been his girlfriend for over a year!

And so I opened the door of the car, got out, and watched him pull away.

Jerk.

I still think about him sometimes, dream about him, long to look at him, touch his tight, hairy butt. Why would I want anything to do with the creep?

I'm deceived, and this is my home sweet home. He intimidates me, but I am more than willing to let it pass, ignore it, welcome his sorrowful apology.

How destructive such forgiveness is when it comes to self esteem and self worth. The forgiveness is in vain if the act of intimidation is repeated over and over again.

Trapping ourselves with a person lethal to our very worth paralyzes us. We will never find our strength, our purpose, and our destiny unless we surround ourselves with positive, uplifting people, ones who nurture us and build us up. Give yourself permission to lose the former lethal people in your life and seek out the latter. Once you find those who will raise you up, hold on tight and start trotting toward your destiny.

Ninety percent of a thing is the realization of that thing. Much of the time we live in an unconscious state of sleep walking through life, allowing "whatever will be, will be."

Are you happy? Are you content with the circumstances around you? If not, you need to wake to a consciousness of your circumstances, analyze, discover, and make adjustments accordingly.

Sometimes we need to pass through suffering, but here's the very important key—do you see hope, growth, and opportunity on the other side of what you are in? If you do, your suffering is reasonable and serves purpose. If you don't, if hopelessness is your only vision, you need to either change your circumstances, or change the way you think and feel about those circumstances.

How do you change your circumstances or your view? By re-writing your perspective of the past or past events, by changing your reactions to circumstances and incidents, by refusing to believe the lies told to you, by scripting a future with characters and belief systems and attitudes that put hope in you—hope that produces determination, and determination that flies you right to your destiny.

~~~~~~~~~~~~~~~~~~~~~~

I search…
Is this my home?
No, too rocky,
But the rocks cool my soles.
Is this my home?
No, too sandy,
But the sand warms my toes.
Is this my home?
No, too grassy,
But the grass is soft under my feet.
Will I keep searching?
Until I again set my feet upon,
That dry, cracked land,
That boils,
That blisters,
That burns?

~~~~~~~~~~~~~~~~~~~~~~

32 *the* FAIRY TALE

There was one thing I always wished for in my life. And I finally did get it.

A home, a husband, and a family.

God did that good sneak-the-nice-guy-in-while-she's-not-looking thing to me, like he did for my mother when he provided my father. He gave this man, who would become my husband, the stomach to bear the sight of my scars.

And with him I'd begin a new life. I left *all* behind—or so I thought.

I prepared for my day—the dress, the flowers, the music. Like almost every young girl, I planned my wedding my whole life.

My day as Cinderella. It's funny because we never do know in the story what the king and queen really thought of Cinderella. We only see their public response, a response which had to be proper.

But what were they saying about Cinderella when the doors were closed? Was it, "Our son? Marry this? This simple peasant girl filled with ashen and soot?" Plus, "Why, he is much too good for a trashy girl like her." Or maybe, "She's disgusting; she comes from filth." And possibly, "You can try and dress her up but she's still no *princess!*"

My future in-laws hated me. I tried not to think about it, but who could blame them? It's the same person who's filled these pages. Any mother would be horrified to have her properly raised son marry someone with a past like mine.

And so it was for me. God gave my husband the stomach, but, for some reason, passed over giving it to the rest of them.

Like I needed more struggle. I was trying to change. Change? I began to wonder if change was really possible?

Growing maybe. We can grow and thus change. But we cannot simply change to be someone we are not. We can just expand on who we are, who we've been. Growth to be pursued through knowledge of ourselves and our fight, not change. We can't change mutation. Its form remains its form. How do we add an arm if there is no arm? Or a leg when there is no leg, or how do we move toes when they are misplaced? How do you miraculously add missing limbs or make things formed a certain way go into their rightful places?

The cells don't move. Remember, they stand fixed.

I have tried. I tried to say to my arm, "Arm, grow an arm," Or my toes, "Toes appear." It doesn't work. My mutation remains.

Acceptance is a powerful tool when it comes to people. We all look for acceptance in one way or another—parents, siblings, co-workers, bosses. Be a carrier of acceptance. Fight each day to uplift at least one person you come in contact with. What you give will spill over and come back to you. Give acceptance, and you will receive acceptance.

My in-laws simply needed to grow. They needed to look upon my scars, spend time with me, and say, "Those scars aren't so bad, she's learned to live with them, she's grown beyond them, she doesn't mind them, and we shouldn't either."

And thus, they allowed themselves to see, touch, and accept my scars, and became wonderfully important people in my life.

~~~~~~~~~~~~~~~~~~~~~~~~~~

Scornful words,
Whispered in secret,
Travel,
Miles and miles,
To the heart of the one spoken about,
They penetrate,
And work to do their job,
Soaking the bones with sadness,
With rejection.
Words,
Words you think are unheard,
Floating through the air,
Causing your victim to weep.

~~~~~~~~~~~~~~~~~~~~~~~~~~

33 *the* DESIRE

I was happy being married. I had married a man who topped all the others I knew. We had just built our first house and just had our first baby together. A boy. A sweet, little boy. I should have been filled with hopes and visions of happiness, but I wasn't. I wanted to die. Every single day I wanted to die.

My daughter was five, about to turn six. Subconsciously, it tormented me. I didn't realize it at the time. That came later—the revelation that when I looked at her, I saw myself and once again felt the little girl I thought I buried long ago arise within me. At the time I didn't know what was happening inside of me.

I asked myself where was this hurt coming from? What was it doing back in the forefront of my head? Confusing me, tormenting my mind?

I watched my little girl when she was with me, and it made me cry inside.

I only cried on the outside when no one was around.

Sometimes my husband found me curled up on the kitchen floor, my arms wrapped tightly around my knees.

No, no, no!

The little girl in me had a voice.

She screamed and cried and cursed. She raged out of control as she banged my head on the kitchen cabinet door desperate to escape the body of the woman who kept her alive. As an adult I understood her need to separate from the pain. She was so small and this pain so large for her to bear. She called out for my help. Help her get away. Kill the pain. I thought of those knives on my kitchen counter. I wanted to grab them. Cut myself up and let the little girl out.

From the outside, it looked like madness. My husband felt lost. He had never seen such a display. The baby was crying, I was crying. Complete turmoil filled his house.

That was not what he expected in a wife—some crazy mutant crying on the kitchen floor. He didn't know what to do. There was nothing he could do. But hold me.

I needed to find my way on my own. Just me and my Maker.

~~~~~~~~~

In darkness,
A tear,
Startling the dry skin,
Moist as the first drop chooses its path,
Preparing the way.
Heated,
As a tiny river forms.
Burning,
As the current rushes forth.
In darkness.

~~~~~~~~~

34 *the* ARGUMENT

Months went by and death occupied my mind. Day after day I argued with death.

No.

I argued with life *knowing* it was death's side I was on. I prepared to kill the pain once and for all. The hurt was too much to bear. Of course I thought of the ones in my life. But they felt like mere needles in my loft full of dirty, dusty hay. When I tried to find the needles, I sank.

The little girl within kept crying to be released. She wasn't obedient anymore. The little, scared, sweet girl turned into one raving mad mess. I couldn't keep her from pounding inside me. Pounding to get out, to be released.

I began to get very upset with this internal battle. Why is she doing this to me? She began to focus on the cause and entertain those thoughts of murder. But she wasn't inside an adult capable of such violence on another person, so she settled on the suicide option.

Arguing with life. Agreeing with death.

It seemed Pain was ready to conquer, once and for all. Or was he?

Things began happening to me. Strange things. Enough strange things I gave "life" one more shot.

I was on my way to a bar to have a couple of drinks before I went to visit my great-grandmother in the nursing home.

I had a notebook in my car. I looked at it, and I had an idea. I parked my car, found a pen and a blank page. I had three questions and wrote them down.

Who, God, are you?

What do you want from me?

Why should I live?

I shut the notebook, pulled from the lot, and drove to the bar.

~~~~~~~~~~~~~~~~~~~

Can You give her wings,
And set her free?

~~~~~~~~~~~~~~~~~~~

35 *the* MESSENGER

My questions got answered, at least the first two, before I even finished my first beer. A messenger. Well, not like some eerie supernatural angel type, but a real person. He answered them for me. I didn't ask for him to. I never said a word about anything. This man walked up to me and started talking. I just listened.

My questions wouldn't have had to been answered that quickly. I wasn't looking for or expecting answers. I actually forgot about the questions. Until I asked "the messenger" why he was telling me the things he was.

"Because God is telling me to," he said.

I raised my eyebrows with doubt about this man's sanity, slammed down the rest of my beer, politely thanked him, and I left. I went to the car and checked my seat. The notebook sat closed. A chill rushed through my spine.

I thought about a couple of other people I knew who experienced "dialogue" with God. They weren't crazy. Was it possible?

I mustered up some faith and began a conversation with Life.

"Why shouldn't I die?" I asked Life.

Because you don't have to.

I heard a voice?

"Why don't I have to?" I wanted to know.

A reply clearly echoed inside of the depths of me,

Because he already did for you.

In all of my arguments with Life, that one had never been presented or voiced to me before. I thought about it. I was speechless, I wasn't sure how to argue that. What if he did?

~~~~~~~~~~~~~~~~~~~~~~

Expectation.
A beautifully wrapped package.
Anxious hands,
Waiting to reveal.
A wishful heart,
Longing to discover.

~~~~~~~~~~~~~~~~~~~~~~

36 *the* BLOOD

There came a point I understood exactly who I came from. Once I was old enough and could bear the stories of generations past, I was trusted with more information. Some of my relatives knew I was tormented and searching. And they tried to help me.

And even with the idea of this chapter, and through a telephone conversation I subsequently took part in, I have just made an incredible discovery. A discovery that came to me just now as I write.

The phone conversation went like this.

"I wonder why Vince shot himself in the head," he said.

Just hearing my second brother's name brought an immediate picture of his lifeless body lying on that cold, steel table, the thought of him brought a sadness to my heart. The caller went on, "If it were me I would shoot myself in the heart."

"Vince's pain was in his head," I said, "yours is in your heart."

I thought about that. Are we subconsciously choosing our action when we have decided to do away with our lives?

"Maybe that's why I always wanted to cut myself up or drink myself to death or gas myself. Because my pain was in my whole body."

I thought it made sense. The kind of pain did match up with the type of suicide chosen. I truly do believe my second brother's torment was in his head. He couldn't seem to stop the voices ringing in his head. This caller would want to shoot himself in the heart for all his pain stemmed from situations with heartbreak.

My mother once shared her suicide fantasy of wanting to step in front of a sixteen-wheeler and send every piece of her body into oblivion, slaughtering every last bit. My own suicidal fantasies involved the whole body, which makes sense; sexual invasion penetrates the whole body. When I think of a victim of rape, what I've seen or heard of it, I see them in the tub or shower desperately scrubbing every inch of their skin. The perpetrator may not have touched their whole body, yet the sexual invasion has affected every inch.

I know it is not just a particular person equals a particular suicide. I endured other frustrations that drove me to want death, situations having nothing to do with sexual abuse, and with those I wasn't inclined to fantasize the same death as I did prior with the sexual abuse pain. These were frustrations and arguments that led me to want to put a gun to my head, or a rope around my neck. I needed to cut off the pain from my ears! Thus I focused on the head.

It would be interesting to test the theory. Maybe I can think of a way to do that some day, or at least keep it at the forefront of my mind when I talk with hurting people. It may even help them to identify their pain, where it lives, and what feeds it. Who knows?

What is the root of my pain?

Sexual sin, maybe the horror and violation of unwanted invasion, the injustice, unfairness. Questions fill my spirit. How does it all come to be? I need answers. I need to understand and find empathy in my heart so I can forgive and move on. How does a person collectively decide to hurt another human being?

At first it is maybe just a thought—a thought that just turns and twists in the head—a secret thought that just wasn't right. And as it is pondered upon, actually entertained by a predator-to-be, it becomes too much to bear. Seducing. Calling. Crying for its release.

Who's calling? Who's seducing?

The beast, a faceless, invisible monster who wanders and searches for anyone he can take over, knocking on the door of a would-be predator until he, the beast, blurs the vision and dulls the senses of his sexual predator-in-training. With success, he creates the molester, the sexual predator, the rapist.

The beast then uses his now occupied, newly formed predator, and draws his prey into a place that is dark, confined, hidden behind closed doors—a place desolate, and surrounded by masses of nothingness, a place that cannot be viewed by anyone who would stop what is about to happen.

Once this beast has feasted through his sexual predator, he will crave for more. The action will get easier as he trains the predator he inhabits to take more and more. It becomes easier to find victims, to lure them, to prey upon them. The victims will be many—the well known number being around one victim of sexual abuse in every four persons—and if a sexual predator makes it a career to satisfy their hunger and fulfill their lusts, just one predator walking the street, working in a school, coaching a sports team, can hurt many. The predator may be one close to the child, the one who gives attention, who nurtures, who seems to care. Why is this person so concerned with my child? Ask yourself; ask your child.

So he feasts, and when this beast has finished with his plattered meal, ready to send his leftovers—the remains of his feasted-upon—carcass through the doors, into the public eye, he stops for a moment. He picks up a shroud from his endless supply of tiffany and hands it to his teary eyed, cut up, wound filled carnage.

And without words, the feasted upon, seem to know exactly what it is he wants them to do with it. Cover up and don't say a word. He has separated from his victims, and they are now left to deal with their wounds.

~~~~~~~~~~~~~

The streets are filled,
Homes are filled,
Neighborhoods are filled,
Cities and nations are filled,
With the ones ashamed,
Blankets twisted around them,
Not to keep them warm,
Or dry,
But covered,
As not to reveal what the beast has done,
What he has caused their souls to become.
And these souls remain quiet,
Unsure why they would protect such a monster.
Afraid,
For their father or mother,
Aunt or uncle,
Brother or sister,
Teacher or pastor or coach,
Husband, wife, or friend,
Fearful there won't be anyone left,
To love,
To be loved by.

~~~~~~~~~~~~~

37 *the* POISON

Incest. Molestation. His participating in, or creating, homosexual orgies at the deer camp. More incest and homosexual molestation.

My mother's father was infected with the evil of all evils. It flowed through his veins and to the very marrow of his bones.

This bothered me, bothered me because *I* had come from him.

I remember sitting in the room of a spiritual counselor my mother brought me to, and saying to the lady, "It's the blood. It's the blood that disgusts me."

I could feel my grandfather's blood running through my whole self. It was black blood, the blackest of black. Evil. Rotten. Running into every organ, every limb, feeding every cell.

And I wanted it out of me. All of it.

That's why I fantasized about the knives and used the razor blades. I wanted to cut myself up and get every drop of black blood out of me.

That's why the slow suicide attempts with the car exhaust and the alcohol. I wanted to paralyze the blood and stop it from living inside me, keep it from flowing through me, keep it from feeding me.

Subconsciously, I knew the path of my pain, the poison that flowed through its trillions of soft tunnels beneath my skin, feeding my disease. This blood was no good. I had to get it out. I had to get *new* blood. I desperately needed new blood.

I panicked over my thoughts unaware my new blood was ever so patiently awaiting me.

~~~~~~~~~~~~~~~

This awful thickness flows through my veins,
I can feel it,
I am conscious of it.
How can I get anything accomplished,
When it makes me so aware it is there?
When will it be as my breath,
And let me live unaware?

~~~~~~~~~~~~~~~

38 *the* CALL

"Where's Jesus?" The office was peaceful, I only heard the voice of this spiritual counselor and my mother's soft breathing from a chair across from me. My eyes were closed, focused on a room that I was seeing. I saw in my mind's eye a scene from long ago.

"Where's Jesus?"

I scanned the room I visualized in my subconscious. I recognized the carpet, a window with its curtain, a dresser, the nightstands, the bed, and the little girl.

No, I wanted to look away from it all. It hurt to look at her, but I couldn't tear my eyes from her.

There she was, that little girl—me, as a little girl. It was difficult to see her. She was covered, with him, the one she named her tormentor.

"Honey, where's Jesus?

I was crying.

"I don't know," I answered, "I don't see him."

The spiritual counselor began to speak firmly at the air. My eyes were closed so I could not see her, but her voice evoked power. And when it did, I saw the one she asked for.

"There. There he is, standing next to the dresser."

He stood there, in my mind, in his amazing strength, almost indescribable in his beauty and power.

"What is he doing?" The counselor asked.

"I don't know," I answered again.

Her commands filled the room and made me shudder. Once again it was as if her commands to allow my mind to be unblinded caused me see.

"He's watching," I told her.

"What else?" She pushed me for more explanation.

I could only shake my head and cry.

I heard my mother's voice as she interjected. "I would think that he would be sad," she offered.

Behind my closed eyes the room I was seeing focused on the corner and then I saw his face.

He was not sad.

He was *mad*.

Mad that he could not stop what was happening to this little girl. That he had no rights. That legally he could do nothing. No one was praying, no one was asking for him to do anything to help this little girl. I had no covering, the covering and protection God promises to those who are his. My roots were evil and he could not impose on a person's free will, a family's free will to choose to live apart from him, from his protection. He could do nothing but watch. And wait.

"What is he saying?" the counselor asked me.

I tried to hear what he was saying. I quieted my insides, slowed my breathing, and calmed my heart. I felt much safer with him in that room.

As I listened to the message he had for that little girl, I began to sob.

Quiet sobs, of joy and comfort, as he spoke, walked over to that bed and lifted that little girl out from under the male body that covered her, freeing her from her prison.

He held her. Held her and rocked her, while whispering sweetly into her listening ear.

What was he saying, you ask?

He was giving her hope. Hope that one day she would be his.

He was promising, with a soft, knowing smile, and a warm touch of his strong hand against her cheek to wipe a fearful tear, promising her *new* blood.

His blood.

Who was he, you ask?

He was Life. The Life I kept pushing aside as I dealt destructively with my pain. His voice was the voice I thought was too painful to listen to, the one I argued with so much throughout my growing days, and the reason I never really let myself unite with Death.

He gave me a message those many years ago, when I was a little girl, tormented in my mind, diseased, masked, twisted in my linen, mummy-like wrappings—a message buried deep inside, waiting to be pulled to the surface.

"Just wait, little girl. Just wait until the day that you will be mine."

What would I be waiting for, you ask?

For Death to be put to death.

Forever.

Inside of me. In my soul, my spirit, my mind, my heart, my very veins.

I waited. And do you know what? He delivered what he promised. Life overcame Death.

~~~~~~~~~~~~~~~~~~~~~

The angels watch,
And they wait,
For soon they know they will rejoice,
For you.

~~~~~~~~~~~~~~~~~~~~~

39 *the* LIGHT

Do you know what happens when Life is allowed to enter the door of your heart in one aspect or area of your life? He begins a work that will leak itself into all areas of our life that hold death. This is what must happen, for death and life cannot reside together—for long. Once the light is placed inside of you, the darkness can no longer stay. Once you flip a switch in a dark room, and the light comes on, the darkness leaves, because it must.

That light you activated, put into motion, will continue to travel throughout the room, to every corner, until the darkness is gone. Think of it not as instantaneous as we see it happen. Instead slow it down and watch the light start at the bulb, its source, and push itself to every inch within that room. Do you see how there is no darkness left to reside with the light?

I visited that house, Trucker Tom's house, the one I lived in when I was a little girl torn from innocence, the one we so abruptly left when they finished the pool. No one was home. I peered through the window not really recognizing the small living room I saw, the stairwell leading upstairs to that bedroom. What jumped out at me was the large family portrait hanging over the stairway. I recognized him, the smile on his face. And there was a boy, about ten. And a girl, about five years younger, blonde hair. And a beautiful wife. This was the very same family I envisioned, stopping me from my murderous fantasies. I could only stand there and cry at the eeriness of it.

The house, the yard, everything was very faint to me. The gate to the fenced-in yard was open, as if it were inviting me in, so I wandered into the back yard. I thought *did I even live here?* I know that I resided here, but did I even live here? I didn't recognize much, but I did remember the pool.

I walked to its edge and looked into the massive concave in the ground. The last time I saw it, it was beautiful, new and full of crisp, clean, pure sparkling water. Now it sat empty, desolate. The liner was torn to shreds, blackness, dirt, and waste covered its bottom. Yuk. I turned my nose up at sight of it all. The beautiful pool turned ugly because it was unattended, overlooked.

It seems the pool and I suffered the same fate within these boundaries. As a small child, I was overlooked, unattended here. When I left, I left with a lifetime worth of dirt and waste, enough to make me live according to the dirt and waste I carried. I viewed myself just as I viewed this pool. Yuk.

But as I sat there and pondered the dirt and waste on the bottom, the torn up liner, the emptiness of the whole thing, I thought, *this is not at all a whole loss.* The foundation is still there; it hasn't changed and the main structure remains the same. The pool could be cleaned up, scrubbed, relined, and made new again. It would just take some time, maybe even a lot of time, but the restored beauty would be worth the effort in the end.

And so, as I stood before that pool, a voice from heaven pointed out that although the pool's fate to become dirty in this place was similar to mine, its potential to be made new and beautiful again was also equal to my potential to be restored, made new and beautiful again.

This is his desire for our lives, the One who brings life, the One who has given us life, the One who *is* life. It's his desire, to wipe out the anger, the unhappiness, the torment. To mutilate it. For good. Forever.

It is very uncomfortable to be set free from pain when it's been with you for so long. I found a sort of comfort living in the pain because I knew it so well. Pain almost becomes a friend, a deceptive friend, but a friend anyway, like cigarettes—you know they are bad for you, but they are always there when you need them. Living with pain is my familiar home, but I'm learning who I really am beyond that pain, without that pain.

But just as it is with the light switch, I don't have to force the light to overcome the darkness; it just happens. I am only in charge of the switch; the rest is up to the force of the light I activated.

And as uncomfortable as it may seem, I do know I will walk off this hard, dry, cracked land once and for all into another—one in which I find comfort, maybe one sandy or one grassy.

We cannot remain in the hallway forever,
A force demands,
A doorknob must be chosen,
A door opened,
A room entered.
One in which a window is found,
With sunshine and a warm, gentle breeze,
In utter surprise,
We catch our breath as we behold,
The amazing passageway through which we may fly free.

BATTLE STRATEGIES
RESCRIPTING YOUR LIFE
the Process and the Potential

We all have enemies. Ones we can see with our eyes and ones we only sense. They are out there preplanning their attacks, what area of our self esteem they will slaughter, and who they will use to do the slaughtering. As a child alone in the world we have little to use to protect ourselves, but as an adult we can gain strength, fight, and conquer far beyond what we can imagine.

We cannot go into battle without a plan or preparation. We need to be mentally prepared to conquer, physically prepared to fight. Strategies need to be at the very top of our lists, easily accessible. Then, once you have developed these strategies to fight oncoming self esteem killers, you will notice yourself spending less and less time down, depressed, and defeated. For us, a human being vulnerable to hurt and pain, we find victory through our fight, through our use of these battle strategies. We find our path, our purpose, and our destiny.

I sit amazed at how I have learned to fight these enemies in my life, how I learned to be free from my circumstances and the circumstances wrought on me by others. We do not have to be connected to these people or circumstances as much as we think we are or are taught to believe we are. We are separate from these incidents; we are separate from these people.

An amazing thing happens when you separate yourself from others and the circumstances wrought in your life by others. It is this. You, as a human being vulnerable to pain and hurt, gain power in your self, power and freedom to be yourself, to live *your* life.

Using these strategies has brought an incredible amount of change in my life. I am happier. My reactions to negative influences around me, judgmental people I come in contact with, have become less and less devastating, almost nonexistent. What may have taken me weeks or months to get over are taking me just hours. It's amazing, so freeing! Here they are for you. Strategize, fight, and gain your victory.

BATTLE STRATEGY 1
RECOGNIZE AND CONFRONT

When I decided I had drained myself of everything within me, I looked at my stack of freshly printed pages and said, "There it is, my story, all of it."

My story. The script I carried with me through the years—years of pain, of torment, of abandonment. Everything that happened in my life I draw from my story. I carried my negative story so closely it leaked itself into every day of my life, telling me who I am, what I can be, how far I can go.

And now it is time to understand, time to heal, time to reach beyond. Because the story I carried was negative, the answers my story gave me were negative. The negative story being losing my daughter; remaining in abusive relationships; deserving words of intimidation giving me negative answers such as *you are worthless, you are nothing and can do nothing*—answers that kept me far from my destiny, my purpose, and my call.

What is your story? The one you repeat every day within the deep recesses of your mind? Your story becomes your defining factor—how you view yourself and your life, your dreams, and your potential to reach your dreams. It is most likely the strongest definition of yourself, your path, and your destiny. Your story dictates how broad or narrow you see your potential, how great or small you see your destiny. It is the story every single friend and family member knows. Even strangers may hear this story.

Now, what are the answers your story brings to your life? What answers does it offer you about who you are, what you can do, how far you can go? If you aren't accomplishing anything, it could very well be your story holding you back. Are the answers negative? Do the answers paralyze you? Set fear upon you? If they do, you must rewrite your story if you seek your destiny.

I said that we cannot change mutation, and I will always believe this to be true. No one should be told that their experiences can be forgotten completely or never felt again, for when the pain is still felt or not forgotten, our first option is usually denial or rebellion, and denial consists of masks and coverings. Remember, our wounds need air. And rebellion brings symptomatic treatment without a thought for the disease. Tackling the symptoms and ignoring the disease carries no real long-term healing.

Our deformities need to be understood and embraced by us, the ones carrying the deformity. And, as with any type of mutation wrought on a person forever growing, learning, progressing through life, we learn to live with, and above, our incapacities. Instead of focusing on our one arm or no toes, we *learn* to live with one arm, or we *learn* to balance with no toes. We search deep and find we are given strengths far beyond our incapacities.

As with any physical handicap, emotional recovery involves *finding* our strengths and *using* them, with determination. One in a wheelchair, if basking in that wheelchair, will never rise. The mind basking in its deformities will never rise above these deformities. The mind basking in its story will never rise above that story.

As with gold, the strength lies deeper within a person. The impurities and deformities on the surface and scattered within can only be removed with the fire. As the fire consumes the deformities, burning them into nonexistence, the beauty and strength of the purer gold can be seen and felt. The goldsmith knows the more he puts his gold through the fire, the stronger and purer it becomes.

Welcome the fire. Allow the fire, the anger, the screaming, the not understanding, and the tears to do their work to burn up your story and everything that keeps that story alive and well within you. Allow the fire to make you stronger, more pure. Allow the fire to make you everything you were supposed to be, with—and beyond—your mutation.

VICTORY: CHANGING MY MIND

I went back to that house with the pool. There was someone I needed to talk to, and by perfect divine destiny, the one I needed to speak to was there. He was one of the main characters in my story. When I look at my story, I see two primary characters. I see him and my mother. My story was usually all about them—the anger, the resentment, the pain was all about them, and how they were the wagons that carried the garbage into my life.

I went because I finally figured out it was time to rewrite my story, that I *could* actually rewrite my story. I spoke with him, my tormentor, for two and a half hours. It was very freeing. I asked questions I needed to ask, and he was more than willing to answer them. And that little girl of his, playing hopscotch? She *is* safe, has always been safe, and seems to have grown into a wonderful young woman that was raised by a loving father. He never took his sexual predatory beyond his adolescence.

I met someone that day who took *his* story and transformed it to make something good out of his life. He grew from his own turmoil, took his own deformities, and learned to find strength beyond them.

The man I sat with on the front step that day wasn't my tormentor any time beyond the time he lived with us as, what he viewed as, a troubled, confused, curious teenager. Talking with him showed me I was my tormentor when I allowed Pain to torment me. All those years beyond my time with him, it was me, consciously deciding I had to live my story, believe my pain. I thought I always had to be pointing at my mutilation; excusing myself from living life because of my handicap; allowing pain to be fed with lies of my own worthlessness, of never becoming anything, or never being loved, because of the deformities.

I saw these were all lies, lies I told myself every day—every day that I wanted to die. I hovered in Death's big deceptive circle, taunted by a beast hungry for his prey. They are one and the same, Death and the beast. The death beast has an agenda for the human being, he has strategies for his battle. This beast first inebriates the unsuspecting, exciting him, arousing his appetite, then inhabits the welcoming. Through this inhabitation, he infiltrates the innocent victim, invites himself into the life of the offended through pain, influences the world to feed the pain, which in turn infects the very breath of a victim until they cry out for their own death. And if that death (or defeat) is accomplished, the circle of the death beast triumphs. The battle of the human being is lost.

Understanding the strategy of your enemy is an immediate victory. It removes his power if you adjust your perception about those that hurt you and who you are and who you have become because of that hurt. Understand it is not personal. It is not human being against human being. It is an unseen enemy who is after your soul, your destiny, your life. And understand from the depths of your heart that this same enemy was once after the one who hurt you, the ones who continue to hurt you. And try to find compassion. For your healing. For with them, he found triumph.

BATTLE STRATEGY 2
REWRITE, REWORK, REFUSE
TO BELIEVE THE LIES

Healing involves finding the way. One in which we throw away the lies and refuse to believe them—the lies told to us and those we make up and tell ourselves over and over until we believe them with our whole heart. We can overcome these lies that tell us we are scarred, and thus we are no good; that with deformity, with mutilation, we are of no use in this world.

Lies—we can refuse to believe the lies and write the stories of our lives differently. We can learn to write defeats as accomplishments. We can learn to view undesirable circumstances as character building opportunities. *Victory is not gained without a battle.* We need to see everything that comes our way, especially the bad and unfortunate, and embrace the opportunity, the purpose, and knowing there is purpose, although it may not be visible, or we may not understand. We let the circumstances make us stronger.

VICTORY: CHANGING YOUR STORY

Now that you have looked at your story, the one you have written for your life, think about how you can change unwelcome circumstances, find your growth, and feel your character grow in something you have struggled through.

What about the story you are helping your children write, or your friends? Every time you are approached, your reaction helps that person write their story. Do you say, "Oh, you poor thing," or, "I know you are strong enough to get through." Look at those two statements and understand *the two different stories a person can write, stemming from the very same circumstance.*

I think my favorite thing about writing is the freedom to create a story and make it whatever I want it to be, to be able to delete and change anything at my whim—to control what is happening, to control how I view something, and how it is viewed by others. I can type, "he was mad," delete it, and type, "he was happy." And just like that I control the story. Media people do it all the time, slant their stories so the stories look how the media want them to. I hope you see how we all do this in our lives every day. How we do this to ourselves. How we do this to others. Ninety percent of the rewriting and growth process is revelation and understanding.

BATTLE STRATEGY 3
THE POWER OF PERCEPTION

We have the opportunity, power, and ability to rewrite our own stories, re-script our lives, and recast our characters.

I've gone back into my story and looked solidly at the characters I developed, and how I over developed them negatively and failed to embrace and write my story around the positive characters who were there and available along the way. I had complete control over all of them. I have written them. I chose to write my mother into my story with frustration and contempt and ignore any of the positive experiences and qualities she may have given me. I chose to continue to write my abuser as the dirtball tormentor he was, for twenty-five years beyond the time I lived with him. I did it in my mastery of judgments on what the characters in my story needed to look, or act, like so my story would accommodate the self pity and self loathing my twisted mind embraced.

VICTORY: CHANGING THE RESULT

We control the perception of our story and its answers in our own mind. We choose to give a situation strength or a certain person power. We choose to put a certain quote by a certain character into the script of our lives. We possess the power for the whole process. Here's how you can attempt to rewrite your story. Beginning with the story you've already written, reformat your perception of the past, sit quietly, and speak these messages deeply within your spirit.

- Begin by deciding to lay out a positive script for your life. If the past is bad or worse, say, *I am prepared to find the good, and receive the positive.* (For example, for me, I needed to realize being a victim had nothing to do with me. I could have been anyone. It wasn't about me or because of me.)

- Tell yourself now is the time. You are independent and will no longer be just a character in someone else's story. (Perhaps you spend time realizing whose story you have placed yourself in: a controlling mother's, or an abandoning father's, maybe an excelling sibling's, or a tormenting abuser's.)

- Slowly help yourself understand you have been going through your life powerless, actually handing over your power by allowing yourself to be a character in other scripts around you written by people who you believed held the power (and more of it) over and beyond you.

- As you meditate your past, recognize the negative and the lies, and prepare to do battle against these lies. Then get your pencil out and be ready to use some tools to re-script your life.

- Convince yourself it is time to break off and write your own, edit your own, produce and direct your own story that you will star in.

I put my belief in this process and convinced myself of my new story, my new past. The circumstances have not changed, for I don't want to live in deception or denial, but my perceptions of my circumstances *have* changed.

What once brought discouragement now brings hope as I choose to view the circumstances as opportunities to build character that results in greatness. This is rewriting my past. First I look at it as I have always viewed it, then I decide every reaction could be changed, and every circumstance could be viewed as opportunity for growth and wisdom. With conscious decision, I have removed the power from my pain, found a new reaction, and thus, gained a whole new perspective. I found a perspective which gains opportunity and purpose which, in turn, accomplishes my needs, my desires, and my destiny.

When you read this chart you will find a circumstance or incident recognized from my story. My negative, old reaction follows with the result of that reaction. See how I decide on a new, positive reaction, and the opportunity it allows me to accomplish something good, something positive. My circumstance hasn't changed, yet look what my perspective does to the reactions to that circumstance. The old reaction brings sadness; the new one, freedom and joy.

Circumstance (Who/What)	Old Reaction (Negative)	Result	New Reaction (Positive)	Opportunity
Possessed by Pain	Suicide	Death or dying	Fight Reach out	Compassion, strength, victory, healing
Childhood memories	Focus on bad	Sadness, loss	Concentrate on positive results	A content inner child, feel loved
My scarred friend's rejection	Disgust, pity	Heaviness, hurt	Give her hope. Share a story of hope for the future.	See a person removed from despair. Gain confidence for self.
Wounds	Shame, cover up, hide	Masks, wrappings, bondage	Reveal, display confidence despite scars	Self-love, strength
Plattered children	Complain of everyone's complacency	Complacency in myself	Be active. Do something to help. Possibly pray for this cause.	Make a difference. Feel useful and needed. Have purpose.
The tormentor, the babysitter	What did I do to deserve this?	Guilt, inferiority	It was not me. It was not about me.	Absolution, freedom
The article, the symptoms	Anger	Resentment, self-loathing	Acceptance	Self-discovery

When I rework my past and remove the negative, I am then ready to script my new life. I can take back my power and write for myself, for my future.

BATTLE STRATEGY 4
BEGIN WRITING

It's a very scary process to stare at a clean white blank piece of paper. It's intimidating and overwhelming. But if we just dive in and start, and remember we are in control of our story, that we are the definers our story, we will write a few paragraphs in no time.

And if the old story starts to appear, we can just go back and delete it while we write a new story, one that contains the premise of purity, goodness, and worthiness. With that we can go on and be everything we were meant to be but were kept from becoming.

Don't fear the white page. Chart your story; see what circumstances you can change to reveal a positive opportunity for wisdom and growth. Watch your dreadful negative hurt, pain, and anger transform to an incredible opportunity for the growth necessary to reach your destiny, to find your purpose.

Seek your old reaction, feel the result. Find a positive reaction, see the opportunity.

Circumstance (Who/What)	Old Reaction (Negative)	Result	New Reaction (Positive)	Opportunity

Spend time with your chart. You have spent most of your lifetime with your negative story. It will take time to soak in the positive. Keep a copy of this chart close to you and when discouragement, depression, hopelessness overcome you, refer back to your positive reaction, get excited for your opportunity. Look at it all as a gift. Nothing is permanent in this life; much can be painful. We cannot remove all circumstances that cause suffering; we can only change our views and our reaction, and thus keep our sanity and our hope.

Once we have reworked our old life's story, changed our thinking, our views, and our reactions to the past, we can start fresh and write the story that will lead us to our purpose and fulfill our destiny. But to do this, we first need a few tools and insight into the process that will create a most successful story.

VICTORY: CHANGING THE MAIN CHARACTER'S PSYCHE

I started my process of analyzing and scripting my own life the same way a writer is taught to analyze and script a character in a movie script or a fiction novel. In my script I am my main character, just as in your story, you are yours. I started with her psyche, her mind and soul. I needed to find her need and her desire, and pinpoint goals to accomplish her need. I understood her need would secretly drive her outward goals.

Every decision you make for your life's script needs to be drawn from your main character's need. You want to see these compliment each other throughout every scene you create for yourself. Your goals can then stem from your deeply buried desire as long as you begin to make yourself aware of your desire, have healed yourself from making goals stemming from negative circumstance, and corrected your perception of past events.

So for her, my main character, if I identify her need as touching the lives of others, I have what I need to create a goal for her, something which will feed her need. She has to feel she accomplished something in direct relation to her need to have satisfaction in herself. With her need to touch the lives of others, it could be as simple and short term as sending her out to smile at five crabby people within an hour, or something difficult and large, like write a book.

Next, you, as the main character, need a mindset or a belief system, with self-talk through which you can achieve your goals.

We do this subconsciously; we choose our attitude about ourselves or society, our beliefs about the world or our own life and those involved in our life, present or past. And some of the time these are in direct opposition to our need, the underlying desire within that ultimately brings us fulfillment and deep satisfaction with life. With that, we create for ourselves a struggle, one that brings disappointment, depression, and other such feelings of hopelessness and worthlessness. This is because we write ourselves with attitudes and belief systems that keep us stuck. Ones that cannot, or will not, help us accomplish our goal, satisfy our need, and reach our destiny.

If, because of a past of intimidation, or simply a present state of acne, my character harbors a belief system that she is nothing, has nothing to offer anyone, that her past or present condition makes her unappealing to the world, how would she ever go about fulfilling her need to touch the lives of others? If my main character embraces a mindset of selfishness, thinking life is all about her and all for her, she will struggle. Her goals will be about herself and her need never satisfied. If my character has inner self-talk that speaks the world is cruel and one person can't make a difference, she will be defeated, and her needs will never be met.

Her mind-set, belief system, and self-talk must line up to create the goals that will fulfill her need. Her need to touch people will only result with an attitude of confidence and boldness. Her belief system must be one that tells her she can make a difference. Her belief system must be that she has a past, present, and future that give her wisdom and understanding to touch the lives of others. Only when her beliefs enable her need will my character accomplish her goals and experience a satisfying journey.

Here's the way I would chart what we've learned about needs, goals, beliefs, and mindsets. Find the complement or contrast to the goals which we have set to satisfy our need. My chart would look like this. I added a "goal met" box. It helps me know I am working on myself and gives me the satisfaction of accomplishment. We all need encouragement, even if we have to remind and encourage ourselves.

Need/Desire	Goal	Beliefs and Mindset in Opposition	Beliefs and Mindset needed to Accomplish Goal	Date Goal Met
Touch someone's life	Help a friend in need	I can't make a difference. What do I know?	I have the experience and wisdom to do something, anything.	4/2
Touch the lives of others	Write a book	Who am I? I can't do that. No one wants to hear what I have to say.	I can do anything. I have value, something to offer. People need to hear my story so they may find hope.	3/17

Notice how I will go nowhere with beliefs and self-talk in opposition to my goal, see the flow and how easy it is to reach my goal when I line my beliefs and my self-talk to accomplish my goal! AHA! Finally!

I also want to give you some examples for people I have run across and spent time speaking with before you chart your own. Once you chart your own, refer back to your chart when you feel you have gotten off track. Record your accomplishments, remind yourself of your victories, and build on your successes.

Need/Desire	Goal	Beliefs and Mindset in Opposition	Beliefs and Mindset needed to Accomplish Goal	Date Goal Met
Security	Save money for 911 situations	I can spend, I'll make more	If I put away $3,000, then I can spend.	11/23
To be loved	Make valuable friends	A little gossip won't hurt	I value a person's reputation.	8/12
To acquire close intimacy with spouse	Have regular meaningful, sexual relations	Sex is dirty, shameful, embarrassing.	My spouse loves me as much as I love him, he wants to be close to me, also.	(Many dates here would be great!)

Here's a chart for your use. Start with your need, then find a goal to complement your need. What are your beliefs? What is your mind-set? Is there self-talk that stifles you from reaching your goal? (You'll usually find this from a past incident that hurt you.) Analyze your negative self-talk, find a positive self-talk, and start meeting those goals that will fulfill your desires today!

Need/Desire	Goal	Beliefs and Mindset in Opposition	Beliefs and Mindset needed to Accomplish Goal	Date Goal Met

VICTORY: CHANGING LIFE'S LITTLE DETAILS

With your main character's mind and soul analyzed, you need to figure out what else your character will have in her life. What will she look like? What will she wear? Write in what you need to, to accomplish these. If you see your character in shape, write in a weekly gym routine, or if you see her getting in shape from being out of shape, remove the daily fast food visits. Remember, you have the power over your script. Does your character bite his nails? Smoke? Drink? Do drugs? Take charge over these details, do with them what *you* choose; you are the one in control. What kind of career will you give her? What hobbies?

Don't forget to line all these details up with your character's need. If my character's need is to touch the lives of others, she may be truly unsatisfied if I give her a career that will not accomplish this.

You will need a setting in which you, your main character, will reside. A state, a city, a neighborhood. Are you currently living in a place you would have written for yourself? Does the place you're living in give you the ability to accomplish your goal and thus, satisfy your need? If not, you need to change that. Maybe it isn't a different city. What about painting a room or clearing clutter to make that home office and accomplish the goal of being organized and on time with your bills, thus fulfilling your need to have peace of mind over your finances?

In keeping with the theme, we'll use a chart. I'll start with a few of the details I listed above and leave room for your own.

Character Details	Goal	Need	What or How	Date Met
Looks like				
Lives				
Does for a living				
Habits				

BATTLE STRATEGY 5
TAKING CONTROL IN CASTING

Next, you need a strong supporting cast, other characters to script into your story. Look around at the people in your life. How do they all affect your need? Your goals? Are they supportive positive characters who help you achieve in life, or are they negative characters who hold you back from what you need to accomplish?

One day I discovered I had control over who is in my life and who is not. For some reason I just thought this was a happenstance thing. I thought just because someone put themselves into my life, they were someone I had to accept. This sort of acceptance was derived from my need to help people. Sometimes our needs allow us to script or cast in a negative way if we don't remain conscious of the result.

If I write about a penniless, hungry character whose need is to survive, I can find him goals that are either positive and productive or negative and defeating. I can have him get a job, or I can have him rob a bank. One goal positive, the other negative; both are derived from the same need.

Imagine a woman whose deep desire is to be loved. Her goals seem to match up with her need. She spends her nights on numerous dates searching for love, and even though she mostly feels unloved, her need drives her out again after each disappointment. With her actions not working, she should analyze and change her script. She could choose between goals of finding "Mr. Right" through numerous disappointing dates, or she could change this to include goals and activities that would push her to spend more time getting to know and appreciate herself, thus resulting in something much deeper and more satisfying—being loved by self. Or maybe she could reach out, help others, volunteer, and thus feel loved by an elderly person or a child versus looking for Mr. Right. Different goals, one just short of achieving the need; the other, achieving and accomplishing. If something doesn't work, if it doesn't feel right, if there is no peace in the situation or the person, change it.

Maybe there is a very rich man whose desire is security. His need drove him to his goal of becoming wealthy, although even with his bank account full, he remains unsatisfied. Why? Because his goal was misaligned with his need. The goal deceived him. He shouldn't stop there thinking he met his goal and thus fulfilled his need. He will only conclude there is no hope for happiness for him. He needs to seek out a new goal. Maybe he takes his money and goes on some personal quest of seclusion in the mountains and finds a relationship with God who will keep him safe, give him protection. He comes back happy, healthy, and invigorated, because he has finally fulfilled the goal that truly satisfies his need: security.

VICTORY: CHANGING LIFE'S CAST

We see how our needs can deceive us into goals that would not satisfy unhappiness, even if we believe our goals are lined up to achieve it. Our cast, the characters we write into our lives influenced by our need, can also be deceived by that same need. The character I used before, the one with the need to touch the lives of others did this.

She welcomed anyone and everyone to take her time from her because her deep desire was to help. Her open door was destructive, for she lost bits and pieces of herself through some of those relationships. One particular relationship that soaked up one-third of her life was derived from her need. She felt obligated to speak with a particular person and do what she could to be a friend to him.

The problem came when this particular person would go into fits of self righteousness and hurt her. He hurt her through his words, his actions. He made her cry and want to put a gun to her own head. Then he would call a few days later and apologize. He always made it seem like it would be the last time. She would give in to this character in her life and allow him to eat up her time, believing she had no choice but to have him there.

And these games went on for years. Things would be fine, and suddenly, he would emotionally slaughter her. Then the apology, and every time she believed the recent attack would be the last.

It was never the last. There would never be a last, ever. She was locked into, what I've called the "battered person cycle." And although the goal and its action were destructive to her self, her life, it was her need that kept her there. What she needed to find was that *she, as her life's script casting agent, has the power to cast her own script!* This particular character needed to be *cast* out of her script. She couldn't help this person and needed to let go and let someone else out there take the position of trying to direct this person.

With this realization, with the recasting she empowered herself to do, she gained an immense amount of freedom to direct herself to constructive casting that would equal or surpass the previous negative attempt to fulfill her need.

Do the characters cast in your life drain you, bring you frustration? Recast. Build yourself a cast who will uplift you, bring you where you need to be to accomplish your goals, and fulfill your need. A recovering alcoholic would need to recast his drinking buddies. A person wanting to move up in the world may need to recast the friends who criticize and ridicule him. A young girl wanting to do well in school may need to recast the peers who would influence her to do otherwise. A person continually brought down by a family member may need to write this person in less and less, or at least balance the script by writing in someone who would equally lift him or her.

Characters, along with the little details your character carries, needs, desires, goals, mind-sets, and a healthy, strong supporting cast are all necessary to write a successful story or script for your life. Work the chart below to understand who your cast is now, and what keeps those characters in your script. Spend time analyzing who will truly satisfy you, your needs, and your life. Who will benefit and who will drain.

Need/Desire	Character	Benefits of Relationship	Drawbacks of Relationship	Actions
To help people	John Doe	I feel needed	I am constantly belittled	Cast out. Don't take calls EVER.
Security	Sally Sue	She's always there for me.	I need to let her know I appreciate her	Cast in. Remember her birthday. Send a card.

After you analyze your own casting chart, take notice that your benefits of relationship align with your need. Notice on this sample chart my relationship with John Doe carries one benefit, but consider it carefully, that benefit does not fulfill my need! In fact, it puts my focus on myself and takes me far from my true need. This will not satisfy me, nor see my goal met. As I weigh the benefits to the drawbacks and find this person spends too much time draining my energy instead of being a positive force which increases my energy while I increase his, I will judge for myself that this is not a character I want or need to script into my life.

Now work on your own characters, you never know what kind of weight you will lift when you remove the "drainers" from your life. And you'll be amazed at the benefit you gain by taking action to remember those so important to your needs.

Need/Desire	Character	Benefits of Relationship	Drawbacks of Relationship	Actions

STRATEGIES UNITED
A FINAL VICTORY GAINED

Your destiny will come. You have a way of catching up with your future, meeting it face to face. Don't let the old story you've lived, or the characters you cast unaware, keep you from your calling in life, keep you from your happiness. Write your story. Then go back and delete. Bring what you need to your story and your characters to correct them in the masterful play you're now creating to expose the new you, the happy you, the successful you. Make your opening night an original—different and fresh. Create an amazing theatrical presentation that hasn't ever been seen before in you.

Work with your old story. Be open to changes you make in rewriting your past to bring positive characterization traits and growth in your character. Let your enemies, your pain, and defeats bring you resolve to battle, to fight for what you need to gain in your life. Then look at your enemies, your pain, and defeats as a means and a doorway to incredible accomplishment and victory. Let go of anything you can't control; release it for good and put your energy in what you can work with, change, and accomplish.

Once you rework your past, you begin to set a new stage for your future.

You sat quietly and found where your need lies. Deep within you, you found the place that holds your desire, your calling, your destiny. You discovered what brings you true satisfaction. Those things that, when accomplished, put a smile on your face, peace in your heart; the needs, that once satisfied, bring content.

You analyzed your belief system, your mindset, what works for you, what you believe about yourself that will accomplish what you need in your life and what you want for others. Your self-talk is now in line with what you need to accomplish in life, to fulfill your purpose.

You created goals for yourself, short and long term ones, I hope, that will satisfy your need for security, love, touching others, or whatever your life's deep desire may be. As you accomplish these, write more goals for yourself that will continue to satisfy your need. Be aware if the goals you spend time accomplishing relate to your inner need, not your negative past, in some way, shape, or form, and with this, you will save yourself from misdirection, discouragement, and depression.

You have analyzed your supporting cast, the characters you will be working with closely on stage. You looked at what they bring to your life. You decided if they complement your need and chose an action to take. Stick with it. Be true to your process and it will work for you. You have started to build a strong supporting cast, removing the characters that bring with them misdirection, disappointment, and sadness. Keep and add characters that bring satisfaction and happiness: ones who drive you to succeed.

Now, present it all on the stage of your life. Present a beautifully transformed drama before the eyes of your assembled onlookers.

Your audience will applaud you—you, as writer, director, producer, casting agent, and star. They will applaud this creation of you that leaves them joyful, filled, and happy.

And for us, who have cried out for healing, who own the process, who dedicate ourselves to our work, we get freedom. Freedom and success. Freedom from all that torments us. Freedom from all who torment us. Success in a life lived abundantly. Success in a destiny fulfilled. Freedom. Success. And life.

ABOUT THE AUTHOR

Tiffany Twist's interest in writing has produced a screenplay and two books. She is now involved in a ghost-writing project, as well as writing a second screenplay. Her second book, *SOME DANCE*, is coming soon.

Tiffany Twist currently resides in Minnesota with her family.